FRANKENSTEIN

NOTES

including
- *Life of the Author*
- *General Plot Summary*
- *List of Characters*
- *Critical Commentaries*
- *Mary Shelley and Romanticism*
- *The Gothic Story*
- *German Expressionism and the American Horror Film*
- *Questions for Review*
- *Selected Bibliography*
- Frankenstein *Genealogy*

by
Samuel J. Umland, Ph.D.
University of Nebraska

Cliffs Notes
INCORPORATED
LINCOLN, NEBRASKA 68501

Editor	Consulting Editor
Gary Carey, M.A.	*James L. Roberts, Ph.D.*
University of Colorado	*Department of English*
	University of Nebraska

ISBN 0-8220-0498-4
© Copyright 1982
by
C. K. Hillegass
All Rights Reserved
Printed in U.S.A.

1991 Printing

Cliffs Notes, Inc.   Lincoln, Nebraska

CONTENTS

FRANKENSTEIN NOTES

LIFE OF THE AUTHOR

Mary Wollstonecraft (Godwin) Shelley was born in August, 1797, the daughter of two notable English thinkers. Her father, William Godwin (1756-1836), was a well-known champion of the cause of the underprivileged. His most famous book, *Political Justice* (1793), is a criticism of existing society as well as an ethical treatise. His other famous book, *Caleb Williams* (1794), has as its theme the privilege of class and the irresponsibility of the aristocracy. It is to her father that Mary Shelley dedicated *Frankenstein*. Mary Shelley's mother, Mary Wollstonecraft (1759-97), was a well-known champion of the feminist cause, and her most famous work is *A Vindication of the Rights of Women* (1792). Mary Wollstonecraft and William Godwin met in 1796 and were married in 1797, in part to protect the legal rights of a forthcoming child – Mary. Mary Wollstonecraft died a few weeks after giving birth to her daughter.

The admiration of the famous nineteenth-century poet Percy Bysshe Shelley for Godwin's *Political Justice* caused him to seek out its author. As a result of their meeting, Godwin began depending heavily on the fortunes of his young poet friend. Although Shelley was already married, he and young Mary Godwin fell in love, despite the objections of Mary's parents (William Godwin had re-married in 1801) and the objections of Shelley's wife, Harriet. In June, 1814, at a time when Mary Godwin would not even have been seventeen, she and Shelley eloped, in company with Jane Clairmont (William Godwin's stepdaughter) on a journey to France and Switzerland. The three returned to England and found themselves mired in scandal; in addition, Shelley faced bleak financial days. The three passed the summer of 1816 in Switzerland, and it was during an evening that summer, while staying in Lord Byron's villa, that the story of Victor Frankenstein first occurred to Mary Shelley. She soon began writing her first work, later to be titled *Frankenstein*.

The return to London in September of 1816 ushered in a series of disasters in Mary's life. One of her half-sisters, Fanny Imlay, committed suicide, and this tragedy was soon followed by the suicide of Shelley's wife, Harriet. Then in June, 1819, Mary's first son, William, died.

Shelley legally married Mary Godwin shortly after Harriet's death, and their fourth child, Percy, was born soon afterward. On July 8, 1822, Mary was confronted by yet another tragedy; while spending the summer in Italy, Shelley was drowned in a boating accident. He was a month short of thirty years of age. Several days after the accident, Shelley's body was washed ashore, and, shortly afterward, in Byron's presence, the body was cremated.

Mary returned to England in 1823, and to her amazement, she found herself a celebrity. *Valperga,* her second novel, was selling well, and *Frankenstein* (1818) had been successfully dramatized.

Among Mary's other novels, *The Last Man* (1826) is of more than passing interest, for it is among the first novels of its kind to treat the notion that human society may someday be destroyed by a pestilence, an idea that today's authors frequently employ – for example, Richard Matheson in his novel *I Am Legend.*

Mary's next novel *Lodore* (1835) is based on the ordeals and frustrations which she and Shelley suffered during 1814; then, in 1836, Mary Shelley's father, William, died, and in 1844, her son Percy, her only surviving child, came into the title of inheritance after the death of her father-in-law, and soon she was able to hand over the task of household management to her daughter-in-law. Mary Shelley herself died peacefully in February, 1851, at the age of fifty-four.

GENERAL PLOT SUMMARY

The outside frame narrator, Robert Walton, writes to his sister about his preparations for an expedition to the arctic regions; later, after the trip is underway, we learn in another letter that the expedition is stranded by enormous ice blocks. While stranded, they see in the distance a strange figure of gigantic proportions being pulled by a dogsled. The next day, an emaciated man is found adrift outside the expedition boat, and he is taken aboard and nursed somewhat back to health. After approximately a week of recovery, he tells the following story to Walton:

He is Victor Frankenstein, and he was born to a distinguished family who were constantly concerned with the welfare of the poor and the underprivileged. When Victor was very young, his family adopted a young girl named Elizabeth, who was raised with Victor.

As Victor was growing up, he was fascinated with varying accounts of alchemy and other related pseudo-sciences, and when he attended the University of Ingolstadt, he began studying all the natural sciences, hoping that he could discover how to overcome death and decay. He began an intense course of study designed to allow him to create life in the laboratory, and finally, after years of intense studying, until he was at the point of injuring his health, Victor was able to collect the various parts of cadavers until he had accumulated enough to create a gigantic creature. Upon completion and upon giving the creature a spark of life, Victor Frankenstein was horrified by the monstrosity of his own creation, and he fled in terror. For a long while, he was sick with brain fever, and for about two years, he knew nothing about the whereabouts of his "creation." However, one day, as he was preparing to return to his family home, he received a letter stating that his young seven-year-old brother had been murdered. The girl who was accused as being the murderess was a close friend of the family; Victor was immediately certain that she was innocent. Intuitively, he felt that the creature whom he had created – and then rejected – was responsible for the murder of his brother. Victor attempted to save the young girl, but his efforts were futile, and she was hanged for his young brother's murder. As a result, Victor felt that he was responsible for the two deaths.

Thus, seeking solitude and the consolation of nature, he climbed high into the mountains and then, suddenly, from a distance, he saw his creature approach him. The creature told how he had survived during the last two years. When Frankenstein gave him life and then deserted him, the creature had great difficulty simply surviving until he found a deserted shack next to the cottage of some poor people; he observed the daily routine of the family through a crack in the wall, and by doing this, he was able to learn to speak and, later, to read and write. After he had learned these things, he accidentally discovered Victor's journal of scientific experiments in the pocket of an old jacket, and thus he learned of his genesis. Now he has sought out his creator for the purpose of asking a favor. Since he, the creature, is so monstrous and so repulsive that he is rejected by all of humankind, he asks his creator to create a companion for him, similar to himself, someone who will not reject him. He promises that if he has a companion, he and his mate will flee from the civilized world and never be heard of again. Victor is reluctant to agree to the proposal, but he finally relents and promises to make the creature a companion.

After renewing his scientific studies in London and elsewhere, Victor settles in a small isolated village in Scotland, where he begins his dreaded and horrible task. As he works, he begins to ponder the consequences of his work, and he changes his mind. He decides that if he creates yet another creature, this one might be even more evil, and, together, the two monsters might begin a race of monsters of untold proportion. He therefore destroys his work, and at the moment of destruction, the creature appears and curses Frankenstein and threatens vengeance, saying that on Frankenstein's wedding night, he will be there to torment him.

Soon afterward, Frankenstein discovers the body of his closest friend, Henry Clerval; Clerval has been strangled. In spite of the creature's warning, however, Frankenstein continues to make preparations to marry Elizabeth, the girl who was raised with him, who has been his lifelong love. On their wedding night, as Frankenstein is securing all of the possible entries to their wedding suite, he hears horrible screams and returns to the bridal chamber to find his bride strangled. He sees the monster fading into the darkness.

Frankenstein pledges that he will follow the monster to the ends of the earth until he can finally find it and destroy it. His pursuit leads him into the arctic regions, where he is taken aboard Robert Walton's expedition ship.

Shortly after he completes his story, Frankenstein dies, and the monster makes an appearance in the dead scientist's room, announcing to Walton that he plans to make a gigantic funeral bier and burn himself in the fire; then he springs aboard an ice raft and is carried away by the waves, lost in the darkness and the distance.

LIST OF CHARACTERS

Robert Walton

An arctic explorer who discovers Victor Frankenstein near death.

Victor Frankenstein

A young scientist; the creator of the "monster"; a modern Prometheus.

Caroline (Beaufort) Frankenstein

Victor Frankenstein's mother; she dies of scarlet fever when Victor is seventeen.

Alphonse Frankenstein

Victor's father; a noble humanitarian.

Ernest Frankenstein

Victor's brother.

William Frankenstein

Victor's youngest brother; he is killed by Victor's "monster."

Justine Moritz

An orphan, adopted by the Frankenstein family. She is accused of being the murderess of young William Frankenstein and is executed.

Henry Clerval

Victor Frankenstein's closest friend; he is killed by the "monster."

Elizabeth Lavenza

A young girl who is adopted by Victor's parents; she becomes Victor's wife and is murdered by the "monster" on her wedding night.

M. Krempe

A professor of natural philosophy at the University of Ingolstadt; one of Victor's teachers.

M. Waldman

A benevolent, kindly professor who introduces Victor to matters "between heaven and earth."

Mr. Kirwin

An Irish magistrate.

The Frankenstein "Monster"

The creature created by Victor Frankenstein; the monster is a victim of misunderstanding.

M. De Lacey

Once an aristocrat, he incurs the wrath of the French government and is exiled.

Felix De Lacey

The son of M. De Lacey; a hard-working, loving son.

Agatha De Lacey

The daughter of M. De Lacey.

Safie

Felix's fiancée; she escapes from her father's home in Turkey and seeks out Felix, who is exiled and living in poverty.

Margaret Saville

Walton's sister.

CRITICAL COMMENTARIES

AUTHOR'S INTRODUCTION (to the 1831 edition)

This introduction, which is traditionally included in every edition of the novel, explains how *Frankenstein* came to be written. The poet Byron, Mary's husband Shelley, Byron's physician Polidori, Mary Shelley, and Jane Clairmont, all figures who were either important Romantic writers (such as Shelley and Byron) or who were close friends or lesser writers, discussed the possibility of writing a horror story. At Byron's suggestion, they all decided to write a ghost story. This was in the summer of 1816. "We will each write a ghost story," said Lord Byron, who began a ghost story which ultimately was never completed, but a fragment is printed at the end of his poem "Mazeppa." Shelley wrote a story based on an incident in his early life, but it is not an important work. Polidori created a vampire story and, hence, in this summer of 1816 two of the most lingering gothic figures in Western civilization were created – the Frankenstein monster and the Vampire figure.

Mary Shelley then tells us that her story was born out of a nightmare that she had. She writes: "I busied myself *to think of a story* – a story to rival those which had excited us to this task. One which would speak to the mysterious fears of our nature and awaken thrilling horror."

Mary began her story on a chilling night in December; at first, it was meant only to be a short story, but at the urging of her husband, she increased the story to its present length.

PREFACE. 1817

Unlike the later Author's Introduction of 1831, this preface was written and published along with the novel in 1817. In it, Mary Shelley refers to a "Dr. Erasmus Darwin" as being a friend of the family (as a historical note, he was the grandfather of the famous evolutionist, Charles Darwin). By mentioning his name, Mary Shelley hoped to give her novel a scientific and a medical credence which it otherwise would not have had. Her real motivation, however, is purely Romantic. She acknowledges that while her story is "impossible as a physical fact, [it] affords a point of view to the imagination for the delineating of human passions more comprehensive and commanding than any which the ordinary relations of existing events can yield." She claims that her novel is "exempt from the disadvantages of a mere tale of spectres" because she intends to "preserve the truth of the elementary principles of human nature." In this statement, she expresses the Romantic desire to delineate the irrational impulses of human nature.

She then relates the events which initiated the writing of her story, and she concludes her preface by stating that "the following tale is the only one which has been completed." With this concluding remark, *Frankenstein* begins.

According to Leonard Wolf, author of *The Annotated Frankenstein*, this preface "was entirely written by Percy Shelley."

LETTER 1: TO MRS. SAVILLE, ENGLAND

The story of Frankenstein and his "creation," his monster, is framed by the story of the arctic explorer Robert Walton. Walton, at present, is in St. Petersburg, Russia, and he is gathering a crew for a lengthy arctic expedition. He relates that it has taken him almost six years to make sufficient preparations for this sea voyage. He has even taken all sorts of physical exercise in order to harden himself for the severe rigors of the cold arctic regions. He also relates that he does not intend to depart for the Arctic until the month of June, but that he does intend to leave for another town very soon. In Walton's concluding remarks, we discover that Mrs. Saville is the narrator's sister, Margaret.

The use of an epistolary story as a frame is an established and clever literary device because it enables the writer to sound more convincing, and it adds another level of verisimilitude. To anticipate the end of the story, this is the person who will actually see the monster; thus, we will, by knowing Walton, believe more readily in the existence of the monster. Certainly in the numerous movies made about Frankenstein's monster, the ending almost always implies that the monster *could* be seen again, someday, in another part of the world. Thus, Mary Shelley tries very early in the novel to make the reader believe that the creation of the monster is possible and that he is, in many ways, almost superhuman.

Since this novel was written by a woman who was in close contact with the great nineteenth-century Romantic poets and whose husband was one of the greatest of the Romantic writers, we can anticipate that this novel will be filled with many Romantic concerns and allusions. Among these Romantic literary practices is, perhaps foremost, the concept of the "Romantic Quest." That is, the frame character here is on a quest for the unknown. Likewise, Dr. Frankenstein will also experiment later with the unknown when he creates his creature/monster. The quest of the Romantic can take all sorts of forms, from Coleridge's "Rime of the Ancient Mariner" (1798) to Byron's "Childe Harold," both of which are poems alluded to during the course of the novel, along with an abundance of allusions to William Wordsworth's poetry.

LETTER 2:   TO MRS. SAVILLE, ENGLAND

In this second letter, Walton tells his sister that he has hired a vessel and has at last assembled a crew, a good crew which, he says, will be able to endure many hardships. He is now in a seaport, Archangel, and he is extremely lonely because he has no friend with whom he can share his Romantic visions nor with whom he can share his enthusiastic response to life. Walton is twenty-eight, unmarried, and he writes to his sister, "I greatly need a friend who would have enough sense not to despise me as romantic, and affection enough for me to endeavour to regulate my mind." Luckily, Walton discovers that the master of the ship whom he has hired is just such a remarkable person; he has an extraordinary mildness of manner, as well as a deep compassion for human emotions. The ship's master was once very much in love with a young girl, but she, unfortunately, was in love with a boy so poor that her father would not consent to the union. The master—although he was deeply in love with girl—could not bear to see her unhappy, and so he bestowed enough money upon the young couple so that they could marry with her father's blessings.

Walton then ends his second letter by describing his feelings on the eve of his voyage to the "unexplored regions" and to "the land of mist and snow" that he will soon encounter. He says that he hopes to have his imagination inspired similar to the best of the Romantic poets because he feels that there is still a "love for the marvellous, a belief in the marvellous, intertwined in all my projects, which hurries me out of the common pathways of men, even to the wild sea and unvisited regions I am about to explore." This statement is the very essence of one of the many facets of Romanticism; it contains a yearning to search for the unknown, coupled with a lure of dangerous oceans and unexplored regions, plus a passionate response to a new challenge, and, finally, it mentions the now-famous albatross from Coleridge's "Ancient Mariner."

It is significant that Walton's inspiration will eventually be echoed by Victor Frankenstein when he desires to create life, because this "god-like" desire contains a concept so lofty and mighty as to awe one. In addition to this parallel between Walton and Frankenstein, Walton's loneliness will also be felt by Victor Frankenstein when he leaves his home and enrolls at the University of Ingolstadt. He will find no other colleagues who are interested in his Romantic pursuits. Solitude is, therefore, one of the strong characteristics of the Romantic inclination; numerous Romantic odes were written to—and about—"solitude."

The mention of the ship's master is not just an accidental fictional touch by Mary Shelley. The story of the ship's master's unrequited love and unselfish generosity expresses the Romantic concern for the lowly and the rustic, and it also focuses upon the sentimental aspects of love—that is, these two young people must have their love consummated at any cost. The sacrifice that the ship's master makes for the young couple is a highly Romantic gesture.

LETTER 3: TO MRS. SAVILLE, ENGLAND

This letter finds Walton well into his voyage. He has now entered the arctic regions, and he is in good spirits, partly because his crew has proved to be a good one. Floating sheets of ice, however, continually pass them. Yet these massive islands of ice do not unnerve or distress Walton. "Success *shall* crown my endeavours," he writes his sister. "What can stop the determined heart and the resolved will of man?"

These enormous, floating sheets of ice once again align the atmosphere of the novel with Coleridge's poem and with other Romantic works, but Mary Shelley's construction is never obvious or mechanical. It is a part of Walton's nature that he *would* notice certain phenomena that another type of narrator would not notice. In addition, these vast sheets of ice also prepare the reader for the later fact that the ship will become stranded due to an enormous ice jam, thereby allowing Victor Frankenstein to come aboard.

LETTER 4: TO MRS. SAVILLE, ENGLAND

This letter is composed of three separate entries. In the first entry, dated August 5th, Walton tells his sister that the ice has surrounded the ship, and he is aware of the severity of the situation. He tells her that they were lost, stranded by plains of ice when suddenly "we perceived a low carriage, fixed on a sledge and drawn by dogs, pass on towards the north at the distance of half a mile; a being which had the shape of a man, but apparently of gigantic stature, sat in the sledge and guided the dogs." About two hours later, the imprisoning ice cracked, and Walton's ship was freed. The next morning, Walton encounters a man who, we learn, has been stranded with his sledge on an ice floe. Before he is taken aboard, though, the stranger asks where Walton's ship is bound, an inquiry which astonishes Walton because the man seems to be nearly frozen, starving, and terribly emaciated. Walton writes, "I never saw a man in so wretched a condition."

After two days, the stranger recovers slightly, and Walton relates that the man's eyes "have generally an expression of wildness, and even madness." Yet if anyone is kind to him, he responds with "a beam of benevolence and sweetness that I never saw equalled." Yet generally, the stranger is extremely melancholy and in great anguish even though Walton feels that "he must have been a noble creature in his better days."

Walton inquires about the reason for the stranger's presence in this isolated place, and the stranger replies simply that he has come here "to seek one who fled from me." Walton tells him that he saw a man the day before, crossing the ice with some dogs drawing a sledge. The stranger's interest is immediate, and he asks a multitude of questions about the route which the "demon" travelled. He is not, we should note, unaware that his keen interest in this creature excites Walton's and others' curiosity; likewise, he knows that they have all been very considerate about his own emotional state. Obviously, this man is a deeply sensitive and high-strung individual.

His health gradually improves, but he remains "very silent and appears uneasy when anyone except" Walton enters the cabin. Already, Walton has begun to love him as a brother, we realize, and we also realize that the stranger's constant, deep grief fills Walton with sympathy and compassion.

The second entry is written eight days later, on August 13; clearly, Walton's affection for the stranger increases every day. In fact, the stranger's health improves greatly, and before long he is constantly on deck, looking out into the vast, empty regions for the sledge that preceded his own. Interestingly, Walton does not yet know the stranger's name nor his story. Yet the stranger is inquisitive about Walton's history, and Walton tells him of his desire to find a friend and of his "thirst for a more intimate sympathy with a fellow mind than had ever fallen to my lot." The stranger understands Walton's feelings, and he tells Walton about such a friend whom he once had but, he says sadly, his friend is now "lost."

The next entry is written six days later, on August 19; the stranger approaches Walton and is ready to explain to him his unique situation. He promises to tell Walton his story the next day.

This section concludes, then, the outside frame, and, at its end, we are ready to hear the story of the stranger who, we will soon learn, will be Victor Frankenstein. Everything about his sudden appearance on the frozen arctic floes of ice, seemingly pursuing something which he refers to as a "demon," prepares us for the fact that the story which we are about to hear will be filled with mystery, bizarre events, and fantasmagoric elements. We are therefore first introduced to the monster – even though we don't know much about him yet, for Walton describes him simply as a "creature of gigantic stature." This is Mary Shelley's clever method of suggesting an objective reality for the monster; this is an aspect which critics such as Muriel Spark fail to consider when they maintain that the monster and its creator are the antithetical halves of a single person.

In a typical Romantic fashion, this concluding section contains a scene in which there is an immediate emotional and an almost spiritual rapport between two sensitive souls, each responding deeply to the other. Walton is sympathetic to the stranger's despair; he sees within the stranger a soul that is "elevated," one that is capable of "intuitive discernment," as well as having "a quick and never-failing power of judgment, a penetration into the causes of things." These and numerous other images come directly from much nineteenth-century British poetry, especially from Wordsworth's "Tintern Abbey," echoes of which we find especially from such lines as "while with an eye/ Made quiet by the power of harmony,/ And the deep power of joy,/ We see into the life of things."

CHAPTER 1

The stranger begins telling his story to Walton even though neither we – nor Walton – knows his name yet. He says that he was born in Geneva, Switzerland, that his family was a respectable one of that republic, always holding some type of public office, and that his father was not married until he was in the decline of his life. The stranger, whom we will soon learn is Victor Frankenstein, feels constrained to tell Walton the history of his father's marriage. One of his father's closest friends, he says, was a merchant who fell from a flourishing business into poverty. He was a proud man named Beaufort, and Frankenstein's father "loved Beaufort with the truest friendship." Beaufort, in his grief, disappeared for months until Frankenstein's father discovered him in a wretched hut. Significantly, Beaufort had a daughter, Caroline, who possessed a "mind of an uncommon mold," and it was she who attended her father with the greatest tenderness during his grief and illness.

Beaufort's health, however, continued to fail, and finally he died. Frankenstein's father, because of his deep concern for Caroline Beaufort, put her under his protection and, after two years, they were married. Frankenstein attributes his father's actions to "a sense of justice in my father's upright mind."

For years, Victor was an only child. But because his parents were enthusiastic travelers and natural humanitarians, a propitious event occurred. During the Frankensteins' numerous travels, his parents would often interrupt their journeys, and due to their "benevolent disposition," they "often entered the cottages of the poor." During one of these visits, in Milan, Italy, his mother found a peasant and his wife taking care of "five hungry babies"; among them, there was a child whom Mrs. Frankenstein found very attractive. This child, says Victor Frankenstein, "was thin and very fair. Her hair was the brightest living gold, and despite the poverty of her clothing, seemed to set a crown of distinction on her head." The girl was a foundling, as it turned out, but was descended from nobility. Victor's parents immediately decided to adopt the child, Elizabeth Lavenza, and, accordingly, Elizabeth became, in Victor's words, his "more than sister," a child cherished and beloved by all who knew her.

Thus, in typical nineteenth-century fashion, the story proper begins with many details about the birth and early years of the main character and with a good deal of background information about his family. But—and this increases both mystery and tension—we have not yet learned his entire name when the chapter ends; all we know is that his first name is Victor. Later on, we will learn that his last name is Frankenstein, a name which is, unfortunately, associated with fear and horror and loathing today. In fact, one of the major misconceptions about this novel is that the name *Frankenstein* is the name of the *monster* that is created. This popular misconception is abetted by the fact that the many movies made about the monster use the name of Frankenstein for the monster. This is a dreadful error; young people today, long before they read Mary Shelley's novel, have the name *Frankenstein* almost indelibly stamped upon their minds as being the name of the monster. It is a shock for most readers when they read the novel and discover that Frankenstein is the name of the *scientist* who created the monster, and not the name of the monster itself.

The intimate friendship between Victor's father and Beaufort, as well as the friendship between Victor and Elizabeth, is emphasized at the very beginning of the novel. Romantic concepts are paramount here, and at the end of the chapter, Victor refers to Elizabeth as being "my more than sister, since till death she was to be mine only." This description correlates the outside frame to the beginning of the story proper since Walton and Frankenstein were also developing a strong emotional bond with one another. Deep friendships will occur again and again in the novel, even until the monster attempts, futilely, to make friends with a humble, rustic family of political outcasts.

Another recurring theme, or idea, which is introduced in this chapter is that of the unfortunate individual suddenly plunged into poverty or tragedy, and then the author allowing us to view that same unfortunate individual being rescued out of poverty. This latter theme is probably due to the influence of Mary Shelley's famous father, William Godwin, whose novel *Caleb Williams* and his tract *Political Justice* are both mentioned in the original dedicatory page. (As a historical footnote, Mary Shelley's name did not appear in the original 1818 edition of the novel.) Likewise, the concern for the poor and the downtrodden, as expressed by the character of Caroline Beaufort Frankenstein, echoes Mary Shelley's own mother's similar concern for the needy and the unfortunate.

CHAPTER 2

Elizabeth and Victor Frankenstein grew up together, and Victor tells us that Elizabeth was a soothing, positive influence on him.

He also tells us that he delighted in investigating "the magnificent appearances of things" and their causes: "The world was to me a secret which I desired to divine."

Seven years pass, and a second son is born into the Frankenstein family; afterward, Victor's parents settled permanently in Geneva. Here, at Geneva, Victor says, it was his "temper to avoid a crowd," and so he was indifferent to his school fellows. We are then introduced to Henry Clerval, Henry's closest and dearest friend. Sharing Victor's interests, Clerval was also concerned "with the moral relations of things." Yet Victor was more concerned with *natural philosophy* due to his chance discovery one day of a volume of the works of Cornelius Agrippa. When Victor's father discovered what his son was reading, he was horrified and admonished Victor severely. Agrippa, he told his son, wrote "sad trash," yet Victor was unconvinced and remained undaunted. Agrippa fired his imagination, and Victor desired to acquire all the works of this author, in addition to the works of Paracelsus and Albertus Magnus.

Victor revered these authors and their ideas, and he became their disciple. For a time, he was occupied "by exploded systems . . . of a thousand contradictory theories." Then, at fifteen, Victor witnessed a huge oak tree blasted by a lightning bolt, and this event caused him to forego his former readings and begin studying *natural phenomena*, especially the subjects of electricity and galvanism, two new and exciting subjects.

Again in this chapter we realize that the subject of friendship is of utmost concern—especially to Victor. His love for Elizabeth and for Henry Clerval filled his youthful days; Mary Shelley emphasizes this deep devotion again and again so that we will better understand the terrible, utter vacuum that will soon be caused in the novel by the deaths of these two beloved friends of Victor. The loss of these two "soul-mates" will be why Victor is reluctant to form another friendship with the frame narrator: for too many years, his passions have been assailed too thoroughly; he can no longer bear to begin a deep friendship with anyone.

The study of natural philosophy would be, in today's universities, the equivalent to the study of natural sciences—that is, chemistry, physics, and anatomy. Shelley's telling us of Victor's imagination, fired by the works of Paracelsus, Agrippa, and Albertus Magnus, is done in order to clearly impress upon us Victor's *inordinate* study of the natural sciences. The eighteenth-century view of these three authors held that they were similar to alchemists—that is, they were people who tried to create life in a test tube or make gold from lead. This will, as a natural consequence, lead to Victor's eventual attempt to create life. And even though the actual creation of the monster is not described, later assumptions hold that the final spark of life came about through the use of electricity—which Victor is now studying. Certainly, the Frankenstein movies all show the use of some type of electricity to create the first spark of life within the monster.

The Romantic concepts expressed in the Faust legend—a legend extremely popular with the Romantics—permeate this entire novel. Man's desire for ultimate knowledge, and the disasters that this desire can have, are two themes that Mary Shelley focuses upon throughout her novel. In this chapter, for example, she writes about Victor's search for knowledge: "It was the secrets of heaven and earth that I desired to learn; and whether it was the outward substance of things or the inner spirit of nature and the mysterious soul of man that occupied me, still my inquiries were directed to the metaphysical, or in its highest sense, the physical secrets of the world." This desire, of course, will lead Victor to commit the Faustian deed of creating life itself.

CHAPTER 3

At seventeen, Victor becomes a student at the University of Ingolstadt in order to be exposed to another type of culture. Before his departure, however, Elizabeth catches scarlet fever; Victor's mother is able to nurse Elizabeth back to health, but, unfortunately, she herself contracts the disease, and on her deathbed, she requests the eventual union of Elizabeth and Victor. This is Victor's first exposure to the death of a loved one, and he laments: "It is so long before the mind can persuade itself that she whom we saw every day and whose very existence appeared a part of our own can have departed forever."

At the time of Victor's departure for the University of Ingolstadt, he is further saddened when he discovers that his closest friend, Henry Clerval, will not be going to the same university. The night before his departure, he gathers his father, Henry Clerval, and Elizabeth around him, all of them seeking repose and happiness. The task is futile, though, and the next morning, he leaves for the University. Victor tells us in detail about his terrible melancholy when he had to leave his home because he was accustomed to being surrounded by his few close friends. For the first time, he is aware that he is completely alone.

On his first day at the University, Victor introduces himself to M. Krempe, a professor of natural philosophy, who ridicules Victor about the books which Victor has been reading, referring to Victor's favorite authors as alchemists and charlatans. Later, Victor meets M. Waldman, a kind and benevolent professor who justifies, in a warm and friendly way, the reasons why Victor should not be concerned with his favorite authors and why he should give his attention to modern discoveries and to modern science; M. Waldman urges Victor to study the modern sciences because "they penetrate into the recesses of nature and show how she works in her hiding-places." M. Waldman's admonitions deeply affect Victor and, thus, under the tutelage of M. Waldman, Victor is introduced to modern science.

Among many other things, this chapter presents Victor's first encounter with death, an encounter that corresponds with his departure for the university, where he will begin his Faustian attempt to create life. The death of Victor's mother is also the first of a series of deaths in the novel which will deeply affect the young Victor. Significantly, death and its ensuing melancholy were the subjects of much Romantic poetry, and as Victor leaves his family and friends, he labels them "old familiar faces," a phrase taken from Charles Lamb's poem "Old Familiar Faces." Lamb, one might note, was a friend of Mary Shelley's father.

Since Victor's new course of studies at the University will eventually lead him to the discoveries that allow him to create his monster, we should note that he is now entering into a deep study of *all* branches of science and mathematics; we can assume, then, that all of his newly acquired knowledge will go into the creation of life, and while the ultimate result will be a *monster*, we must remember that the creator is *not* a "diabolical scientist"; instead, he is a highly moralistic and altruistic person.

CHAPTER 4

In this chapter, Victor begins his studies of the natural sciences, particularly chemistry and anatomy. M. Waldman becomes a true and helpful friend, and Victor's studies improve considerably. After two concentrated years of study at the university, Victor masters several subjects perfectly. During these two years, however, he has not paid a visit to his home in Geneva.

A recurring question that he asks himself is: "Whence . . . did the principle of life proceed?" In order to properly examine the causes of life, he studies death by closely observing the natural decay and corruption of the human body. He maintains that during the time of these events which he is narrating, he was *not* a madman; he simply spent an inordinate amount of time with his studies, and he was given over to total solitude: "I shunned my fellow creatures as though I was guilty of a crime." As a result of his total devotion to his studies, he succeeds in "discovering the cause of generation and life . . . [and he] became capable of bestowing animation upon lifeless matter." He is aware of how dangerous his knowledge is becoming, but he is adamant in his desire to create life from inanimate matter. He is aware that his first efforts might be imperfect, and because he cannot work with all of the minute aspects of the human torso, he decides that he will create a figure of simplified, gigantic proportions. "Pursuing these reflections, I thought that if I could bestow animation upon lifeless matter, I might in process of time . . . renew life where death had apparently devoted the body to corruption."

In his pursuits, Victor was, in fact, following the admonitions of Professor Waldman: "I pursued nature to her hiding-place." He admits that he saw terrible horrors as he "dabbled among the unhallowed damps of the grave . . . [and] collected bones from charnel-houses . . . [until finally his] eyeballs were starting from their sockets in attending to the details of my employment." He likewise intends, in a "god-like" way, to "animate the lifeless clay." He spends the entire summer engaged in this *Promethean* pursuit – to the complete neglect of his family, not even answering their letters. In fact, he works in complete solitude, shunning *all* of his fellow students. By the fall, he hopes that his creation will be complete.

Thus, this chapter further emphasizes the Romantic Quest. Earlier, Walton was embarked on his own Romantic search into the Arctic; now we see that his kindred spirit, Victor Frankenstein, is embarking on a most explicitly Faustian search for the very meaning of life – indeed, for life itself. We should remember, at this point, that the subtitle of this novel is "The Modern Prometheus." We see, there-fore, in this chapter the beginnings of the Promethean theme of the novel—that is, the bringing of life, and light, into the world. In classical mythology, there are several myths about Prometheus, but the most frequent is that after the creation of other things, man was created last and was given fire as a means of protection and light. Traditionally, Prometheus is seen as a friend of man and as his pro-tector, and, in some legends, he is viewed as the creator of man. The reader should also be aware that the Romantics were exceptionally fond of the Promethean theme, and the title of Percy Shelley's greatest drama is *Prometheus Unbound*. Not surprisingly, then, Victor Frankenstein, in attempting to create life, uses his Promethean talent not only as a gift for man in order to create life, but, likewise, to con-quer death. This theme is similarly woven into the Romantic Faus-tian legend, because Faust devoted himself to the pursuit of *all* knowledge in order to conquer death and to understand all life.

Victor's inordinate amount of study, combined with his shunning of his fellow students gives us a complete, composite picture of the Romantic solitary wanderer, a fictional figure who was popular in all Romantic literature. In contrast, in popular cultural renditions, Frankenstein is usually portrayed as a "mad scientist." It is important, therefore, for today's readers to realize that Mary Shelley definitely does *not* intend for the reader to see Victor as *mad*; to the contrary, Victor's quest is to rid the world of death, an altruistic and noble motive.

CHAPTER 5

This chapter focuses on the completion of Victor's creation. As soon as the creature comes to life and Victor looks into its eyes, he is horrified at what he has done. The yellow skin of the creature barely covers the muscles and arteries underneath. Its eyes are watery and horribly yellow and are hardly distinguishable from the sockets in which they are set. Victor has worked for two years on this "creation"; he is disgusted, mortified, and horrified of it, and he im-mediately abandons it in total dismay and horror, aghast at the frightening "thing."

Later, when the monster visits him at his bedside and attempts to speak, Victor rushes from the house and once more flees in bitter disappointment of the creature and himself. He is haunted by the creature's presence, and he desperately fears that it will approach him again. He is literally sick with fear, and he dares not look about him. He is reminded of the passage from Coleridge's "Rime of the Ancient Mariner" in which the Mariner feels isolated from the world.

In Victor's confused, aimless wanderings about the city, he is thrilled to suddenly meet his old dear friend Henry Clerval, who has just arrived from Geneva. Henry tells him that Victor's family is fine, but that the entire family has been very concerned about Victor's health. The two then return to Victor's apartment, and Victor impulsively begs Clerval to save him from the monster. Clerval attributes Victor's mutterings to the onset of an attack of some sort of brain fever, and, indeed, soon afterward, Victor does become very ill, and for several months he lies half-conscious, with Clerval as his only attendant. Then, as Victor is recovering, he receives a letter from Elizabeth.

In Mary Shelley's original concept of this novel, this chapter was meant to be the original beginning of a work that would have been much shorter than the present novel. After she was persuaded to lengthen her initial work, however, she went into far greater detail concerning Victor's creation of the monster and his subsequent horror and disappointment.

Clearly, Victor's desire for knowledge has led him to the very limits of human understanding. And as Victor's attitude toward his "creation" changes, so also does our opinion of Victor change. He totally rejects his own creation, a project upon which he labored for a very long time. His reputation, at this point, seems excessive; can the creature really be so horrible? After all, it was created from once-human limbs. As a result, however, of Victor's absolute rejection of the creature, his repulsion becomes, ironically, a complete reversal of the Romantic Quest.

The monster is presented as having a natural love and respect for his creator, as is evidenced by the monster's approaching Victor's bed. This scene will become even more important later because the monster himself will reveal that he was not *originally* either violent or vicious. Also too, the monster will later reveal that he wants only to be treated as a human being. This chapter, then, is the beginning of Victor's disclaiming attitude toward the creature, and it also contains the initial stages of the monster's being forced to live completely devoid of all kinds of human companionship.

The relationship between the scientist and his creation is a difficult one. Several critics have discussed the antithesis between Victor and his creation, and while this was a valid concern of many Romantic writers, it does not seem to be the main purpose of this particular novel. Instead, Victor's rejection of the creature, and its subsequent alienation and loneliness, is Mary Shelley's primary concern; in fact, this theme is as valid a Romantic concern as is the split, or double, personality interpretation of the novel. In conformity with the typical gothic novel, the creation of the monster occurs during a thunderstorm, late at night, and by candle light. This "laboratory" is apparently located in some isolated part of an old house. Thus, the environment, within the framework of the traditional Romantic concepts, reflects the state of the heart and mind of the creator, as will later be seen when Frankenstein confronts the monster among the jagged rocks and peaks of the mountains. Here, too, the emphasis will be on the darkness of the surroundings, which will be correlated with the brain fever which Victor falls prey to later.

The reference to Coleridge's "Ancient Mariner" in this chapter is important. It indicates that like the Mariner, Victor experienced a yearning for the Romantic Quest, and now he is haunted by his new knowledge. His original quest was to create life, and once that feat was accomplished, his quest became, ironically, his *curse*.

CHAPTER 6

The letter from Elizabeth causes Victor to become extremely homesick: the children are growing and everyone is fine; Ernest is now sixteen and wishes to be a soldier, and Elizabeth says that she feels that it is necessary to tell Victor about a girl named Justine Moritz. Elizabeth then recounts for her brother the events by which Justine entered the Frankenstein family, and her story about Justine turns out to be very similar to Elizabeth's own story. Justine's entire family died, and since there were no surviving relatives, she came to live with the Frankensteins, and soon everyone became very attached to her. Young William Frankenstein, who was just a baby when Victor left for school, is now about seven years old. Elizabeth then turns from family news, and she shares with Victor some gossip about the people in Geneva, stories which evoke pangs of nostalgia in the recuperating Victor. Ultimately, because of Elizabeth's letter, Victor improves.

When he feels sufficiently recovered, Victor introduces Clerval to various professors at the University, and everyone praises Victor for the astonishing progress which he has made in the sciences. Clerval is pleased. And thus the days pass pleasantly, and soon summer is gone, and Victor prepares to return to Geneva in the fall; yet the harsh early winter prevents his going, so he and Clerval remain in Ingolstadt.

The following spring arrives uncommonly late, yet by May, Victor and Clerval are wandering about the environs of the city, and the spring air seems to have greatly revived Victor. "My own spirits were high, and I bounded along with feelings of unbridled joy and hilarity," he says.

In this chapter, Mary Shelley does not concern herself with the whereabouts of Victor Frankenstein's monster; it is as though the monster, after he was rejected by Victor, simply disappeared. Likewise, she does not concern herself too much with chronological accuracy. There is, for example, an apparent contradiction, or omission, concerning the age of young William and how long Victor has been away at the University, but this point is not of central importance.

The story of Justine Moritz curiously parallels Elizabeth's own history, and, therefore, once again, we encounter a concern for the downtrodden and for the victim of adversity. The Frankenstein family's charitable concern for Justine is a harsh lesson to Victor, who has recently neglected his scholastic and familial duties to carefully and laboriously create the monster.

CHAPTER 7

In this chapter, Victor receives another letter; this one is from his father, and it contains dreadful news: young William Frankenstein has been murdered. Victor's father relates that the family had been walking in Plainpalais, a region south of Geneva, when William became inexplicably lost. The family assumed that he had probably gone home, yet when they returned, they discovered that he was not there. In panic, they went searching with torches for the young boy, and early in the morning, they found him, with "the print of the murderer's finger . . . on his neck." Victor's father pleads with his son to return home immediately to be with them. Victor is deeply disturbed by the terrible news, and he makes immediate plans to return to Geneva. Clerval is helpful and comforting as he helps Victor make preparations to set off on a long, melancholy journey back to Geneva. It has now been six years since Victor has been home, and he realizes that his pleasant, once anticipated homecoming has now been utterly destroyed.

Crossing the lake to Plainpalais, he sees a storm approaching over the summit of Mont Blanc. Against the rocky shore, the lightning illuminates "a figure which stole from behind a clump of trees . . . [and] lightning illuminated the object, and discovered its shape . . . . its gigantic stature," and its hideousness betrays to Victor that it is "the filthy demon to whom I had given life." Victor immediately intuits that what he sees is the monster, his creation, and that the monster is the murderer of his brother. Two years have passed since he created it, and he feels now as though he is responsible for releasing into the world "a depraved wretch, whose delight was in carnage and misery."

Early the next morning, Victor arrives at his father's house and finds his father, his younger brother Ernest, and his cousin Elizabeth all in anguish. They tell him that Justine Moritz has been accused of William's murder. Victor refuses to believe the accusation, and Elizabeth is also convinced of Justine's innocence. The Frankensteins intend to put their faith in the laws of their country, for they are all convinced that Justine will be found innocent.

The key incident in this chapter is, obviously, the letter from Victor's father, Alphonse, announcing the death of young William Frankenstein. The letter instigates the second part of the novel's plot. That is, until now we have been almost wholly concerned with the creation of the monster. Now we will begin to see the effects that the monster will wreak on Victor's life. Significantly, it is ironic that Victor's first deciding to study the natural sciences at the university was caused when he saw lightning strike down a huge oak tree; consequently, we assume that the monster's "life" was somehow activated by lightning, and now, after two years, lightning reveals to Victor the presence of the monster in the area where young William was killed. Additionally, it is also a part of the Romantic tradition that Victor is able to immediately intuit that the *monster* is the *murderer* of his young brother.

Victor's conviction that every human being is guiltless is an indication that, in his own mind, the monster is *not* human. However, as we later learn, the monster *does* possess all of the basic human emotions, and, moreover, we should remember that the monster was not created innately evil. The evil which he exhibits was acquired as a result of Victor's rejection of him.

CHAPTER 8

All of the evidence against Justine is circumstantial, but nevertheless it proves to be ultimately convincing. During the trial, it is discovered that Justine was seen by a townsperson early in the morning, not far from the spot where William's body was found. It is also revealed that a servant of the Frankenstein family found a picture (a locket) in Justine's pocket, which Elizabeth had placed around William's neck shortly before the Frankensteins set out for their walk. Justine, in her defense, admits that the evidence indeed points to her guilt, but she strongly maintains her absolute innocence. She tells the jury that she had intended to pass the evening of the night of the murder at her aunt's house, but on her return, a villager mentioned William's disappearance, and she therefore spent several hours looking for him. By the time she finished her search, she discovered to her dismay that the gates to the city of Geneva had been locked; thus, she had to spend the night sleeping in a barn next to a cottage. She awoke early the next morning, and it was then that she was seen by the villager. As for the matter of the locket, she cannot account for its presence in her pocket. She can only conjecture as to how it came into her possession. Several witnesses are then called to attest to the goodness of Justine's character, and they all speak well of her. Elizabeth Frankenstein is one of these character witnesses; she maintains Justine's innocence before the court, but the public is convinced of Justine's guilt.

Victor passes the night in wretchedness, and next day, he learns that Justine has been unanimously condemned to be hanged. Elizabeth is distraught and wails, "How can I ever again believe in human goodness?" Justine expresses a desire to see Elizabeth, and Victor accompanies his cousin to the jail. There, Justine admits to them that she did finally confess her guilt, but she did so only to gain absolution; had she not done so, the priest who attended her threatened excommunication. She tells them, though, that she *is* innocent. Tragically, there is absolutely nothing that anyone can do now to save

Justine, and the next morning, she is hanged. Victor says sadly, "William and Justine were the first hapless victims to my unhallowed arts."

Returning to the matter of Justine's description of how she spent the night outside the locked gates of Geneva, this description should be kept in mind because later, when the monster explains his actions after he murdered William, Justine will become, for the reader, a Rachael-type figure as she weeps over the death of a child whom she loved deeply. In fact, *Justine*, her name, is Mary Shelley's ironic wordplay on the term "Justice," since Justine is the first victim of a gross *in*justice. Victor's realization that legal and moral justice has been perverted is the reason for his deep, anguished sorrow and horror, as will be more clearly seen in the next chapter. The natural order of things has been destroyed – all because of Victor's creating the monster; as a result of his quest to discover all the secrets of nature and create life itself, he created a monster who, because of society's rejection of him, became corrupt and turned to murder and, as a result of coincidences, caused the hanging of an innocent young girl, Justine Moritz.

CHAPTER 9

The deaths of William and Justine affect Victor so deeply and emotionally that he cannot recover his health nor his sanity. He enters into a state of deep despair and depression. He is almost mentally annihilated by the extreme remorse which he feels for having created a monster who became the instrument of death for two beloved people. Victor's father tries to console his son, but Alphonse does not realize that all of his advice to Victor is "totally inapplicable to [his son's] case." Victor's despair is so deep that it brings him to the point of suicide, but only the fact that his death would bring additional grief to his beloved Elizabeth restrains him from taking his own life.

Despite everything, Victor cannot escape from the continual mental horror of the realization that *he* is "the author of unalterable evils." "I lived," he says, "in daily fear lest the monster whom I had created should perpetrate some new wickedness." He has a strong intuition that the monster will indeed commit additional monstrosities. Victor reflects on all that has happened and realizes that because of all his "crimes and malice," his "hatred and revenge burst all bounds of moderation." Finally, he feels that he would like to see the monster again; in this way, he might "wreak the utmost extent of abhorrence on his head and avenge the deaths of William and Justine."

In addition to Victor's emotional trauma, Elizabeth is also extremely despondent; when she thinks about the deaths of William and Justine, she can no longer view the world with the sense of justice that she once possessed. She knows that William was *murdered*, and she is certain that Justine is *innocent*; therefore, the real murderer is still alive – and free.

Victor realizes that he cannot always cope with his anguish, and so, to restore his sick soul, he decides to make an extended trip through the beautiful valleys of the Alps, where the magnificence of the scenery will, hopefully, become a restorative to his troubled spirits. Thus, he sets out and soon he arrives at the village of Chamounix, where he takes a room; he rests in his room and watches the pallid lightning flashes that play above Mont Blanc and, finally, sleep comes to his troubled soul.

In this chapter, Mary Shelley focuses on despair and depression, common subjects for most of the Romantic writers of her time; in much nineteenth-century Romantic poetry, the characters often entertain thoughts of suicide – indeed, suicide was prevalent among a good number of major and lesser Romantic writers. Poems such as "Ode to Dejection" and similar poetic cries of despair were common characteristics of Romantic poetry. The Romantics were aware, however, of the theological implications of despair, for which there was no forgiveness because such emotionalism would often lead to suicide. Victor's despair and his consideration of suicide is an ironic aspersion on his youthful aspirations if we remember that, initially, he once desired to overcome death by *creating* life.

Here, for the first time, Elizabeth laments the existence of injustice in the world. This concern for injustice is also one of the Romantic writers' primary concerns. Mary Shelley's own father, William Godwin, had written on political justice, and his influence can be seen in many aspects of this novel.

It was also commonplace for the Romantics to take solace from natural scenery and nature. Accordingly, Victor returns to the mountains and streams, as well as to the lakes and valleys which he once visited six years ago. There, we find more echoes from Wordsworth's

"Tintern Abbey"; in that poem, the troubled poet returns to Tintern Abbey after five years, and he brings his sister with him because he hopes that the scenery there will restore their troubled spirits. In terms of the plot of this novel, Victor's desire to rid himself of his depression will lead him, later, to an actual face-to-face confrontation with the monster.

CHAPTER 10

Victor goes to the mountains because, he says, "these sublime and magnificent scenes afforded me the greatest consolation" that he was capable of receiving. They had the effect of soothing his grief and calming him, and, to some extent, they diverted his mind from the thoughts about which he had been brooding.

One day, during a vicious rainstorm, he ascends to the summit of Montanvert. The precipitous terrain is full of jutting rocks, and broken and blasted trees litter his path. Falling boulders echo through the ravines, and the rain falls in torrents. Victor laments that he is a thinking being; to him, it seems as if it would be better to be a beast of the fields, one with no concern whatsoever. He is reminded of favorites lines from one of Percy Shelley's most beautiful poems, "Mutability."

Victor continues his climb, and by noon he is at the top of his ascent, and he relaxes by sitting atop a rock in a sea of ice. The face of the glacier reminds him of a troubled and turbulent sea. For a moment, he forgets his heavy despondency, and his heart swells with joy. He says, "Wandering spirits, if indeed ye wander, and do not rest in your narrow beds, allow me this faint happiness, or take me, as your companion, away from the joys of life." At that moment, a figure appears in the distance, moving toward Victor with "superhuman speed." It is Victor's creation, his monster, and he screams, addressing it as a "devil" and as a "vile insect."

Much to our surprise, the creature does not savagely strike Victor, nor does he react with hate; instead, he answers Victor philosophically: "All men hate the wretched; how, then, must I be hated, who am miserable beyond all living things!" The creature laments that he is detested even by his creator; he recognizes that Frankenstein wishes to destroy him. Therefore, he reprimands Frankenstein by asking, "How dare you sport thus with life?" The creature begs Frankenstein to hear the details of his plight and hear what has happened to him since he was created—and rejected. The creature admonishes Victor by saying: "Remember that I am thy creature; I ought to be thy Adam, but I am rather the fallen angel, whom thou drivest from joy for no misdeed. Everywhere I see bliss, from which I alone am irrevocably excluded. I was benevolent and good; misery made me a fiend."

The creature's desire to be heard is sufficiently tantamount that Frankenstein finally consents, and the two retire to a hut on the mountain, where Frankenstein begins to feel "what the duties of a creator towards his creature were." With this, the creature begins his tale.

Clearly in this chapter, we see that in contradiction to all popular conceptions of the Frankenstein story, here is a creature/monster who is philosophical; that is, he is able to evoke the image of God, the story of the Creation, of Adam as the first man, and of the fallen angel, Lucifer. The creature, responding to his rejection by his creator, speaks of his miserable condition which, theologically, is a comment upon the Romantic concept of the fallen state of man. One of the chief concerns of the Romantics was the relationship between man as a divine being and the Creator as a divine entity. We are being prepared here, though, for a reversal of the Romantic concept because God did banish Adam from the garden of Eden, but God *never* referred to Adam as "abhorred monster! Fiend that thou art!" The concept of rejection, of course, is here, but Mary Shelley makes an analogy of the creature with the fallen angel and to Adam's being banished from the garden of Eden. We must remember that it was indeed God the Creator Himself who placed the Tree of Knowledge in the Garden, and it was from the Tree that Adam ate; God was also responsible for putting Eve in the garden. But in paralleling God and Victor Frankenstein, Mary Shelley makes it clear that the creature was created with noble intentions and that he was good until he was rejected. Adam violated Divine Law. The creature violated no law; he was rejected without reason, and as a result of Victor's irrational rejection, it was "misery," the creature says, that made him a "fiend." He tells Victor, "Make me happy and I again shall be virtuous." The creature also says that his *soul* was essentially benevolent, and that, initially, upon his creation, he "glowed with love and humanity."

Victor has obviously created a being with vast powers of reasoning and sensitivity.

Again, this is the basic Romantic concept: man is born innately good and virtuous. Opposed to this point of view is the view of many religious sects. Some religious sects, for example, hold that man is born in a state of depravity and is naturally sinful. This is *denied* by the monster, concerning his own genesis; the monster was forced into his evil habits by the state of society in which he has lived. As Rousseau pointed out in his theories about the "noble savage" – and certainly the monster is a noble savage archetype – man is born innately innocent and good. It is the *institutions of mankind* that create evil.

The relationship between the creator and his creation (his creature) is pictured here rather unusually – that is, the creature is the more humane of the two, and it is also the creature who expounds the Romantic concepts. It is also the creature who talks of love, goodness, and compassion. It is, thus, the essence of Romanticism to have such a creature state philosophically, "believe me, Franken- stein, I was benevolent; my soul glowed with love and humanity." Not surprisingly, throughout the chapter, the emphasis, besides be- ing on the physical aspects of the mountains and the serenity of the natural world, emphasizes again the Romantic aspects of the novel, focusing on the goodness of the creature before it was corrupted by society.

As noted above, everything that we see in this chapter about the creature contradicts the many horrible characterizations of the monster in movies, plays, and novels. We are now prepared to enter into the story of the creature after he was rejected by his creator.

CHAPTERS 11-16

The next six chapters, unlike the popular concepts of the hideous Frankenstein "monster," constitute the very moving story of a crea- ture created and immediately rejected; they focus on his attempts to become a "humane" creature (or human), and the essential import- ance of these chapters lies *not* in their intellectual or literary concepts but in the simple and moving narrative which the creature narrates. To the uninitiated, this is the most surprising aspect of the novel – that is, the creature's response to life.

It was, we learn, with considerable difficulty that the creature first responded to life. He had all of the sensations of a fully grown individual; he had a sense of smell, sight, hearing, feeling, and taste, but he had not gone through the maturation process. When he was rejected by his creator, one of his first sensations was that of intense *light*, and he remembers how difficult it was for him to see. Later, after he fled, he saw a dark forest near Ingolstadt, but he realized that he was tormented by hunger and thirst, yet confusion and despair overcame him finally, and he fell asleep. Without understanding why, he soon knew that he was "a poor, helpless, miserable wretch. . . . I could distinguish nothing; but feeling pain invade me on all sides, I sat down and wept." He found a huge cloak (Victor Frankenstein's) which he covered himself with, and, dumbfounded, he watched the sun go down and "the orb of night" come up.

One day, he found the remnants of a fire that had been left by some wandering beggars, and he was delighted by the experience of warmth, but, painfully, because of his lack of knowledge about the world, he put his hands into the fire. Because of this, he quickly learned the value and the power of fire, and, along with this, he discovered how to dry some branches in order to keep the fire going. He also discovered that the fire gave off light at night.

One of the most difficult things that the monster learned was how to find food. Some days he could find nothing but acorns to assuage the fierce pangs of hunger. Then, propitiously, after spending some time in the forest and woods, he discovered a small hut, which was a new sight for him, and it aroused his curiosity. When he entered the hut, he found an old man preparing his breakfast. The old man looked up and fled in abject horror. This was the creature's first realization that his appearance was one that was horribly different from that of other members of humanity. Looking around, he realized that the hut was appealing, and he consumed the remainder of the peasant's breakfast; then he left the hut and noticed how many other houses were close by. Once when he entered a small village, he was subjected to abuses, both physical and mental; for that reason, he found it necessary to take refuge in the forest. He realized anew that he was outside the benefits of the community and was rejected by man. At this point, he found a cottage which had an adjoining "lean-to" with an earthen floor, but despite its crude accomodations, it was "an agreeable asylum from the snow and rain." He was happy to find a shelter—"however miserable" from the inclemency of the season and *still more from the barbarity of man"* (emphasis ours). Contrapuntally to the popular concepts of the monster, we see that Mary Shelley is emphasizing that the creature's inhumanity is directly related to the inhumane treatment which the creature receives from the community of man.

Next morning, the creature discovered that he could live in the lean-to structure and, moreover, that he could perceive through a crevice the behavior of the inhabitants in the cottage. Remembering the barbarous treatment which he received the night before, the monster decided to isolate himself for some time. In fact, regardless of the lowliness of his surroundings, he found it to be "a paradise compared to the bleak forest [with] the rain-dropping branches and the dank earth." Peeking through the crevice into the main house, he was able to discern an old man and a young couple who played music on some unknown instruments and sang sweet but mournful songs.

Night came, and the creature was astonished to see that the people inside the cottage had ways of illuminating it by means of candles and lamps. Also, in addition to the beautiful sounds of music which the creature heard, he also heard what he later discerned to be the family's reading poetry and other literature.

After the family put out the lights, the creature also went to sleep; he was in complete amazement that such a type of life existed. But having developed an almost instantaneous sensitivity to human relationships, he perceived that the three peasants were not happy. "I saw no cause for their unhappiness, but I was deeply affected by it. If such lovely creatures were miserable, it was less strange that I, an imperfect and solitary being, should be wretched"; it was sometime before the monster discovered that the cause of the family's unhappiness was poverty. Yet he noted their generous acts of goodness; for example, the young people often went without food in order to give enough to the old man. "This trait of kindness moved me deeply," he says, because he had been stealing from them, and he realized that in doing so, he "inflicted pain on the cottagers." So, instead of stealing, he returned to existing mainly on his former diet of wild berries, nuts, and fruits. Once again, we must be aware that Mary Shelley is creating a type of Rousseauean natural man, one whose first response to human beings is that of sympathy and compassion. Mary

Shelley's intention is clear: if Victor – or others – think of the creature as being an evil monster, *we* should realize that evil is *not* an innate quality within the creature's personality. In fact, after realizing the dire poverty of the cottagers, the creature would often take tools and would do their work for them during the night, while they were sleeping.

It was not long before the monster realized that the young couple were a brother and a sister, named Felix and Agatha; he could not ascertain the old man's name, however. The old man was simply referred to as "father." Gradually, the monster began to learn to do different sorts of work, and, in addition, he learned the value and use of bread, milk, and wood; the creature also began to listen with intensity when either the brother or the sister was reading to the father; at first, he was puzzled, but then he discovered that there existed "paper signs for speech," and he wanted to approach them so that he might learn, but he was afraid that "the deformity of my figure" would frighten them. He had become "fully convinced that I was in reality the monster that I am." This was a bitter realization for the creature, and he decided to apply himself as thoroughly as possible and learn to speak.

When spring came, a lady came to the cottage, and Felix, the brother, was obviously deeply enamored of her; he embraced her and called her his "Arabian." When night came and the ladies retired, Felix called her his "sweet Safie." The days passed, and as the family and Safie continued to converse and read, the monster listened keenly and "improved in speech and also learned the science of letters, as it was taught to the stranger [Safie]." As Felix instructed Safie in various matters, the creature learned in secret also, and when he learned of the discovery of the American hemisphere, both he and Safie wept "over the hapless fate of its original inhabitants." This is Mary Shelley's comment on Rousseau's "noble savage" concept. In fact, this concept was a key concern of the Romantics; they looked upon the noble savage as a creature in direct communication with God and the natural forces of the universe. This is an ironic comment, coming from the mind of a creature who has been so completely rejected by his creator. In fact, after hearing the story of the fate of the American Indians, he pondered: "What was I? Of my creation and creator, I was absolutely ignorant . . . but I knew that I was imbued with a figure hideously deformed and loathsome." Yet, at the same time, he monster says, "I admired virtue and good feeling and loved gentle manners and amiable qualities." Nevertheless, he realized that he was a miserable wretch. He had no friends and no mother nor father; he did not have his creator near him, and he had no one to bless him with "smiles and caresses." As a result, he watched the happy family, and he began to admire them and love them deeply. Thus, we will see that in the early stages of the creature's history, he was a creature of gentle emotions, capable of human love and in need of human companionship; he deeply felt his own isolation and the inhumanity of the world toward him.

It was still some time, however, before he learned the peasants' language well enough to know the history of the family, who were named De Lacey. It is a typically Romantic story: the De Laceys were descended from nobility, and Safie's father had been a Turkish merchant (Safie was Turkish) who had lived in Paris for years; he suddenly incurred the wrath of the French government for some unknown reason and was jailed. Felix De Lacey happened to be at Safie's father's trial and was incensed by the political injustice of the proceedings. He decided to visit Safie's father, and it was during that meeting that he met Safie and fell deeply in love with her. Safie's mother was a Christian Arab, a detail which is a typically Romantic twist. Later, Felix and Safie became engaged, and Felix helped her father escape from jail, but the French government soon discovered Felix's role in the escape and, as a result, the entire De Lacey family was deprived of their fortune and were exiled. It is because of these unfortunate circumstances that they came to live in Germany. Meanwhile, Safie's father took her back to Constantinople, but because she had been reared by a good Christian mother, Safie resolved to return to Felix as soon as possible. Taking some expensive jewelry with her, she made her way to Germany and then to Felix's hut.

When the creature heard this story, he was deeply moved; he suddenly looked upon crime as a distant evil. "Benevolence and generosity were ever present before me," he says. Once again, we must point out that according to the Romantic view, goodness is natural and evil is a result of the institutions of mankind.

One night, while trying to find some food, the creature discovered a leather portmanteau containing several books, and among the books which he found were Goethe's *Sorrows of Young Werther*, a highly romantic work; Milton's *Paradise Lost*, which deals with man's creation and fall and eventually with his reunion with his creator; and Plutarch's *Lives*. As he read *The Sorrows of Young Werther*, he was thrown into frequent spells of depression, but Plutarch's work taught him positive thoughts and elevated him "above the wretched sphere of [his] own reflections, to admire and love the heroes of past ages." How extremely different this concept of the creature is from the usual Frankenstein monster which we have encountered in the movies. To this creature, reading *Paradise Lost* was one of the most moving emotional experiences he had ever encountered. The monster responded to "every feeling of wonder and awe that a picture of an omnipotent God warring with his creatures" was capable of exciting within him. The basic similarity between the creation of man and the creature's own creation struck him profoundly, and he realized that, like Adam, he was united to no other being; many times, he wondered if Satan might be a symbol of his own condition. Like Satan, he too was rejected by his creator.

One day, by accident, the creature discovered some papers in his pocket, and since he had learned to read, he discovered that he possessed the journal which Dr. Frankenstein kept during the four months previous to his creating the monster. Thus, the monster was able to track down Frankenstein, and, using the analogy from *Paradise Lost*, the creature realized that he had no Eve to soothe his sorrows or share his thoughts: "I was alone," he says, and "I remembered Adam's supplication to his creator. But where was mine? He had abandoned me, and in the bitterness of my heart, I cursed him." Thus again, throughout this narrative, we become ever more responsive to the creature's isolation, his rejection, and his abandonment than we do to Frankenstein's feelings.

The creature quickly realizes that the small De Lacey family has much more concern for each other than Frankenstein has for him. They are truly good people, and so the monster decides to approach M. De Lacey. The old man is blind, and the creature reasons that perhaps since the old man cannot see him, he will not be repulsed by the monster's appearance. So, one day while the young people are away, he takes a chance and tries to talk with old M. De Lacey. The old man is responsive, and he agrees with the monster that "to be friendless is indeed to be unfortunate." He deplores prejudice, and he praises brotherly love and charity. As the two begin a conversation, and old M. De Lacey is responding to the plight of the stranger, the young people suddenly return home and discover the monster with the old man. Seeing the hideous creature, Felix, with almost supernatural force, manages to tear the creature from the old man. The creature could easily have killed Felix, but, overcome by despair and anguish, he rushes from the cottage.

The creature then ceases his story and turns to Frankenstein and cries out, *"Cursed, cursed creator!"* Continuing his narrative, the creature says that he then left the cottage and, "like the arch-fiend, bore a hell within" him. From that moment on, he declared himself to be at war with mankind. We have seen in this story which the creature narrated to Frankenstein that he was essentially a child of nature, seeking goodness, love, and compassion, but that the prejudices of mankind caused him to become the personification of evil. Furthermore, it was upon reading Frankenstein's journal that he discovered that Frankenstein was not only his creator but also his "father," in a sense. It is incomprehensible to him that a father could so callously reject his own creation. He sees Frankenstein as an "unfeeling, heartless creator." He tells Frankenstein: "You endowed me with perceptions and passions and then cast me abroad as an object for the scorn and horror of mankind." In his determination to discover his creator, his search and his suffering have been long. For example, during his travels, he rescued a young girl from death, but when the girl's father saw him, he tried to shoot the creature. The creature's reaction was this: "So this is the reward of my benevolence." "The feelings of kindness and gentleness," he says, which he had entertained only a few moments before gave place to "hellish rage and gnashing of teeth." It was then that he vowed eternal hatred and vengeance on all mankind. Thus, the evil of the monster is born as a result of the evil of mankind toward him. Again, we perceive the Romantic point of view: evil is not innate in the heart of man; it comes from man-made prejudices.

The creature finally arrived at Geneva, and there he saw a beautiful child; thinking that the child was too young to have developed a prejudice against ugliness, he approached him with love. Yet the boy was horrified and cried out, "Monster! Ugly wretch!" Then the young boy revealed that his father was named Frankenstein, and the creature became so incensed that he murdered the child. This child was young William Frankenstein, for whose death Justine Moritz was hanged. The monster explains how he placed the locket which was around the neck of the young boy in the pocket of a young girl whom he found sleeping in a nearby barn. The creature tells Frankenstein that he is now "alone and miserable. Man will not associate with me. But one as deformed and horrible as myself would not deny herself to me. My companion must be of the same species and have the same defects. This being you must create."

As we come to the end of the creature's story, we realize that he is a person of extreme passions and in extreme need of companionship. (As a footnote, the creature's desire for a mate was responsible for one of the greatest horror films of all times – *The Bride of Frankenstein*; see section on "Filmography.") Here, it is important to note that everything about the creature's story is at variance with today's general concept of what – and who – the monster is. His association with the De Laceys, also victims of poverty, is important to Mary Shelley's political purposes in the novel, and Mary Shelley now moves from being concerned with a basically compassionate creature to one who will become a vindictive, murderous monster, but we must remember that it is *society's* rejection and scorn of the creature which cause this metamorphosis.

CHAPTER 17

It is again emphasized in this chapter that the monster *demands* a female with whom he can live in an interchange of sympathies and compassion. Mary Shelley makes no mention of sexual implications, but, instead, she emphasizes the sympathy and companionship which the monster desires. This same need for companionship was the subject of Walton's letter to his sister in the beginning of the novel. Frankenstein, however, immediately refuses the creature's demand, but the creature tells him that "I am malicious because I am miserable . . . and you my creator should pity me." The monster emphasizes that he needs a creature of the other sex, just as hideous as himself. He assures Frankenstein that while he and his bride live, they will not be happy, that they will live a life that is harmless and free from misery, and, furthermore, no human beings will ever see them again. They will leave civilization and live in the wilds of some South American country. For a moment, Frankenstein's heart and feelings are filled with horror and hatred, and yet he recognizes that he does owe his creation something. He finally consents to the demands of the monster, holding him to his promise that he will never be seen in a civilized country again.

The creature warns Frankenstein that Frankenstein's whereabouts will always be watched by the creature and that when Frankenstein begins making the companion, he will be ever-present, always watching.

CHAPTER 18

Here, Frankenstein realizes that he cannot create another "creature" without months of laborious study. Thus he again falls into a deep, brooding melancholy, and even his trip into the lake country and into the mountains does not rid him of an extreme depression. Frankenstein's father recognizes his son's depression and, fearing for his mental health, he suggests that Frankenstein and Elizabeth be married. Victor assures his father that he loves no one else as much as he loves Elizabeth, and he fully expects to marry her, but not in his present state of mind. Obviously, he cannot tell his father that his objection to an immediate marriage is due to the fact that he feels bound by a solemn oath to create another being, a mate to his previous creation; afterward, he can then "let the monster depart with his mate before [Frankenstein] allowed [himself] to enjoy the delight of marital bliss." He is also aware that all types of accidents could occur to hinder his creation of a companion for the monster, and, in addition, he does not know if the project will take months or years.

It is at this time that he discovers that his father and Elizabeth have arranged that he should spend some time in England; there, he can spend his days and nights reading about the latest scientific discoveries. Henry Clerval is to accompany him on his journey. He travels to Strasbourg, where he meets Clerval, and they begin their journey to England. On their way, Frankenstein is tremendously affected by the scenery, and once more he is reminded of passages from Wordsworth's famous Romantic poem, "Tintern Abbey."

London, then, is to be their place of rest. Clerval wants to meet some of the great minds of the time, but Victor feels that he himself will not be able to respond to people because he is "sealed with the blood of William and Justine." After spending several months in London, they receive an invitation to visit some friends in Scotland. Clerval is eager to accept the invitation, and Victor says, "although I abhorred society, I wished to view again mountains and streams and all the wondrous works which nature adorns her chosen dwelling places." This is yet another echo from Wordsworth's "Tintern Abbey."

CHAPTER 19

The two friends set out, beginning a journey that takes them through England; they spend a considerable amount of time at Oxford, and then they travel north, to the various lakes of Cumberland Westmorland; as they approach Scotland, Victor often has the strange feeling that the "fiend"—his creation—is following them. They visit Edinburgh, and after a week, Victor tells Clerval to enjoy himself because he has to be alone for awhile. "I may be absent a month or two; but do not interfere with my emotions, I entreat you; leave me to peace and solitude for a short time." Again, this is the Romantic expression of the importance of solitude. In actuality, Victor wishes to isolate himself, to discover some remote spot in Scotland and finish his work in solitude. As noted in the later section of these Notes, "Mary Shelley and Romanticism," Switzerland, the Rhine, and Scotland were often favorite settings for the Romantic writers. For example, Poe, in "Ligeia," has his narrator leave the Rhine when his beloved dies and enter an abbey in the most remote part of Scotland. Here, Mary Shelley has Victor travel to one of the most remote parts of Scotland, where even the soil is barren. On the island which Victor inhabits, there are only "three miserable huts," and he rents one which contains only two rooms. Shortly thereafter, he begins his work, an attempt to create a second creature, a female companion for "the fiend." Victor is terribly repulsed by his new endeavor, however, for unlike his earlier desire to create life, now he dreads this new task. "Sometimes I could not prevail upon myself to enter my laboratory for several days, and at other times, I toiled day and night in order to complete my work." It was, indeed, a filthy process in which Victor was engaged. Often in the midst of his labors, he would assiduously avoid all human contact, and he often questioned his work with "obscure forebodings of evil that made my heart sicken in my bosom."

CHAPTER 20

During the creation, Victor remembers that it was only three years ago that he was engaged in the same kind of work, and then, after months of hope, he tragically realized that he had created "a fiend whose unparalleled barbarity had desolated my heart and filled it forever with the bitterest remorse." Now he realizes that he is about to create a similar being, and he suddenly realizes that, in addition, "she" could become even more malignant, murderous, and wretched than the creature which Victor has already created. The male creature *promised* to quit the region and never be seen again, but how can Victor be sure that this *new creature* will comply with the monster's conditions? He is aware that the monster which he has already created despises his own deformity; what if the female creature, given the female's predilection for beauty, is even more dismayed by her deformity, thus becoming even more depraved? And then another terrible possibility occurs to Victor: what if these creatures should procreate an entire race of "monsters"?

While Victor is meditating on these horrible conjectures one evening, he looks up and, to his horror, the creature peers at him through the casement of the hut: ". . . he had followed me in my travels, he had loitered in forests, hid himself in caves, and taken refuge in wide, deserted heaths, and he now came to mark my progress and claim the fulfillment of my promise." After Victor sees the creature, he knows for a certainty that he cannot continue his work, and so he tears to pieces the female creature that he was working on. Outside, the monster lets out "a howl of devilish despair" and disappears into the night.

In a Romantic, gothic novel, we should not be concerned with verisimilitude. That is, we should not ask, *how*, on a deserted island, Victor gathered together enough pieces of enough cadavers to create the female monster. Mary Shelley never bothers to explain; thus, we should not question; we should continue with her narrative. First, we learn that several hours later, Victor heard the opening of a door, and the creature was suddenly before him. He tells Victor of the terrible miseries which he has endured; he wonders now how Victor can dare to destroy all of his hopes. Victor responds: "Never will I create another like you, equal in deformity and wickedness." Here, we should remember that the wickedness which Victor speaks of comes from the abuses which the monster suffers because of society's attitude toward him; evil does *not* form a part of the monster's basic character. Because Victor will not create a mate for him, the monster howls, "You are my creator, but I am your master;

obey!" This is a forewarning that the monster will strike out against Frankenstein, and that he will create for him a monstrous hell. In biblical fashion, the creature asks, "Shall each man find a wife . . . each beast have his mate, and I be alone?" Carrying through with the biblical analogy, the creature warns Frankenstein that he "will watch with the wiliness of a snake, that I may sting with its venom." It is then that he threatens Victor, saying, "Remember, I shall be with you on your wedding-night." This threat will, of course, be fulfilled in a later chapter.

Victor tries to attack the monster, but the monster eludes him and, finally when he is alone, Victor remembers only the monster's phrase *I shall be with you on your wedding-night.*" Being unable to sleep, Victor returns to his laboratory and takes the remains of the "half-finished creature" that lie scattered on the floor and disposes of them by taking them out to sea. As he throws the pieces into the sea, he feels that he is committing a dreadful crime. His mind is in such a state of confusion that he decides to remain out at sea for a long period of time. Being totally exhausted, he falls asleep. When he awakens, he finds that the wind has driven him far from the coast, and he is terrified. Hours pass before he is able to return to shore. When finally he does manage to steer his boat into a harbor, a group of people immediately surround him and take him to Mr. Kirwin, a local magistrate.

Victor is now in Ireland, and the townspeople demand that he account for his presence because a gentleman was found murdered in their village the previous evening. The chapter concludes with Victor's statement, "Little did I then expect the calamity that was in a few moments to overwhelm me and extinguish in horror and despair all fear of ignominy or death."

CHAPTER 21

In the office of the magistrate, Victor listens to the testimony of several witnesses concerning the murder which occurred the previous night. It seems that three men were fishing the night before and, putting into port, they discovered that they could not land at the harbor, and thus they had to moor their boat about two miles up-stream. It was there that they stumbled upon the body of a man on the beach. He had apparently been strangled: ". . . there was no sign of any violence except the black mark of fingers upon his neck."

After several more people testify, Victor is shown the body. It is the lifeless form of Henry Clerval. Victor becomes hysterical and has to be carried out of the room in convulsions.

For two months, Victor lies ill, on the verge of death; he calls out, again and again, for his lost friend. When he finally awakens and gains consciousness, he finds himself in prison, and even though he is being attended by gentle people, he is overcome by gloom and misery. Even Mr. Kerwin is kind to him, extending his sympathy and assuring Victor that he believes that Victor is innocent. One day, Victor's father arrives and tells Victor that the family is fine; Victor's sickness abates, and he realizes that he has spent three months in prison. Eventually, he is acquitted of the murder charge, and he makes immediate plans to return to Geneva. There are now three deaths that have been perpetrated by Frankenstein's monster.

CHAPTER 22

Victor feels that he has unleashed an abhorred enemy among the people he knows and loves; thus, he gives himself over completely to solitude and despair—despair caused by his tragic realization that young William, the "poor, unhappy Justine," and now Henry Clerval "all died by *my* hands" (emphasis ours). By this, Victor means that it was his hands that created the monster and, therefore, he feels personally responsible for all these deaths. Sometimes in his sleep, he unconsciously cries out his feelings of guilt, saying such things as "I am the assassin of those most innocent victims; they died by my machinations." It is his guilt because he created the monster that troubles him so terribly.

After a considerable passage of time, Victor finally becomes calmer, and before he leaves Paris, he receives a long letter from Elizabeth Lavenza, in which she states that she releases him from all obligations of marriage, realizing that in his years of study and travel, he has probably found someone else whom he wants to marry; she is sure that by now Victor is willing to marry her only because he feels duty-bound to honor his commitment of long ago. Her letter reminds Victor of the monster's threat: *"I shall be with you on your wedding-night!"* In spite of the monster's warning, however, Victor decides to marry Elizabeth, anyway; he hopes that, somehow, their marriage will bring happiness to her and also happiness to his father. He writes to Elizabeth and tells her that he has a dreadful secret which he will reveal to her, but he warns her that it is truly "a tale of misery and terror," one which will "chill your frame with horror." A week later, Victor and his father return to Geneva; Elizabeth is shocked at her fiancé's emaciated frame and feverish cheeks.

Soon afterwards, the marriage between Victor and Elizabeth is arranged, and once again the threat of the monster causes Victor to lapse into a terrible depression, yet he continues to make preparations for the wedding, and we learn that a part of Elizabeth's inheritance has been restored to her by the Austrian government. Until this moment, we have not had any indication that Elizabeth had an inheritance, yet it is a part of the Romantic tradition to introduce the unexpected.

As his wedding day approaches, Victor takes several precautions. He obtains pistols and daggers to protect himself and Elizabeth from the monster. His mood is anxious, and even Elizabeth finds herself growing melancholy in anticipation of the dreaded secret which Victor promised to tell her. On the day of the wedding, they stop for the night at Evian, planning to continue their wedding trip the following day.

CHAPTER 23

The ceremony over, the newlywed couple does not reach their hotel until eight o'clock in the evening. A strong wind and storm descend upon them, and a thousand fears gather within Victor. In a gothic novel such as this, it is often common for the author to insert incidents taking place during violent thunderstorms, and the following scene is no exception. Victor is extremely agitated by the dark, threatening weather. Elizabeth begins to retire for the evening, and Victor searches all the passages of the house, "inspecting every corner that might afford a retreat to my adversary"; he can find no traces of the monster. Suddenly, however, he hears a shrill, dreadful scream from Elizabeth's room. He rushes to the room, and his worst fears are manifested. There is Elizabeth, "lifeless and inanimate . . . her bloodless arms and relaxed form flung by the murderer on its bridal bier." Victor falls senseless to the floor. When he recovers, he finds himself surrounded by other people in the inn, and once again he sees Elizabeth's body. He rushes to embrace her, but the "deadly languor and coldness of the limbs" make him realize that Elizabeth is dead. He rushes to the window, and there he sees the monster in all of its abhorred hideousness. Staring at him is "a grin on the face of the monster." Victor recoils as he sees the monster seemingly jeering, his fiendish finger pointing towards the corpse of Elizabeth. Victor fires a pistol, but the monster eludes the bullet and disappears into the night.

The crowd in the inn joins Victor in an attempt to find the monster, but all their tries are futile. Victor becomes ill and has to be taken back to the hotel; he is shocked beyond belief at what has happened and horrified that the death of his beloved wife has been added to the deaths of William, Justine, and Clerval, all victims of the monster. He wonders if it is possible that the monster is now attacking his father or his brother Ernest. His creation has destroyed all of his hopes of happiness, and even though it is difficult to relate his narrative, Victor reveals that "one by one my friends were snatched away; I was left desolate."

Victor's father and Ernest are alive when Victor returns to Geneva, but grieving over the death of Elizabeth, Victor's father soon dies of grief, and when this happens, the collective deaths of young William, Justine, Elizabeth, and now his father are simply too much for Victor. He goes mad and is kept for a couple of months in a solitary cell. Upon being released, he appears before a local magistrate and tells him about the murderer of his family. At first, the magistrate does not believe Victor's incredible story, even though he is attentive and interested. Finally, though, he tells Victor that if such a monster exists, he does not have sufficient power to capture it, for a creature such as Victor has described "can traverse the sea of ice and inhabit caves and dens where no man would venture to intrude." Victor is certain, however, that the monster is hovering close by, and as he leaves the magistrate, he tells him that his hatred is "the devouring and only passion of my soul," and that he shall devote the rest of his life to realizing the final destruction of the monster which he created.

CHAPTER 24

Victor leaves Geneva and begins his quest to destroy the monster. He travels throughout most of the world, enduring unbelievable hardships. The intensity of his revenge is the only thing which keeps him alive. Yet, before leaving Geneva, he visits the cemetery where Elizabeth, his father Alphonse, and William are buried, and he realizes with new horror that their murderer is still alive. He once again makes a solemn vow to destroy the fiend, and as he makes the oath, he is "answered through the stillness of night by a loud and fiendish laugh." The monster is concealed, but Victor hears it say very clearly, "I am satisfied, miserable wretch! You have determined to live, and I am satisfied." Victor dashes to the place where the voice seemed to emanate, only to see the monster's "ghastly and distorted shape as he fled with more than normal speed." He has pursued the monster constantly since then. He saw the "fiend" hide himself in a vessel bound for the Black Sea, and even though Victor took passage on the same ship, he could not discover the whereabouts of the monster. As he pursues the monster from country to country, he is aided by villagers who have seen or heard of the monster's presence. Sometimes the monster has left messages on trees and rocks, urging his creator to follow him: "I seek the everlasting ices of the north where you will feel the misery of cold and frost to which I am impassive." Again, Victor vows never to give up his chase until either he or the monster perishes. And when the monster leaves a note stating that Victor should provide himself with heavy furs and food, Victor procures a sled and dogs in order to pursue the monster more easily to the arctic regions. By now, he has lost all sense of time; he is not even aware of how many weeks or months he has pursued the monster. Often the monster allows Victor to see him from a distance, only to quickly disappear. Once Victor was able to come within a mile of the monster, yet when he was almost within grasp of his enemy he "lost all trace of him more utterly than [he] had ever done before."

After several of his sled dogs had died, and Victor was about to yield to death, it was then that he saw Robert Walton's vessel. Victor tells Walton that he has restored Victor's health and now that that has been accomplished, Victor realizes that his life's task is unfulfilled; he must continue his search for the monster. Victor tells Walton that if Walton should ever see the monster, he should destroy him because the monster's "soul is as hellish as his form, full of treachery and fiend-like malice."

WALTON, in continuation
TO MRS. SAVILLE, ENGLAND; AUG. 26

Walton's next letter is dated a week after his previous one, and we are now again in the outside frame, narrated by Robert Walton. Walton writes that this strange and terrifying story might not be believable, but that everything – the anguish in Victor Frankenstein's voice as he told his story, the letters of Felix and Safie which were shown to him, and the apparition of the monster, seen by Walton himself – all of these things convinced him of the truth of Frankenstein's narrative. Walton tried to get particular information about the creature's physical creation, but on this point, Victor was impenetrable. When Victor discovered that Walton had written down the entire story, he read the narrative himself and made corrections. Walton also writes about the great sensitivity and the lively wit of Frankenstein and also of his great intelligence; obviously, he found Frankenstein to be "an admirable being, the kind he had long sought as a friend." Walton wants to reconcile him to living a positive and productive life, but Victor maintains that too much has happened to him, and that no one can ever be the close friend to him that Henry Clerval was, nor can anyone equal the beloved companion that Elizabeth Lavenza was. Victor says that his destiny is to "pursue and destroy the being to whom I gave existence; then my lot on earth will be fulfilled and I may die."

TO MRS. SAVILLE: SEPT. 2

In a brief letter to his sister, Walton lets her know that he and his crew are again surrounded by mountains of ice and that they may never escape the dreadful situation. (These letters, incidentally, were not actually mailed at the time of their composition; they were stacked away and mailed later.) Walton is terribly depressed by the weather's hindering his mission, and the super-sensitive Frankenstein tries to assuage Walton and to lift his spirits.

TO MRS. SAVILLE: SEPT. 5

They are still surrounded by ice. Frankenstein has declined in health, although there is still a "feverish fire" that glimmers in his eyes. The other news is that the crew of the ship has come to Walton and has asked for assurance that if the vessel is freed, they will not pursue the quest into the arctic regions any further – a request to which Walton agrees. Frankenstein, however, is horrified that Walton should so easily put aside his quest. Frankenstein says to Walton, "are you so easily turned from your design? Did you not call this a glorious expedition?" As a point of characterization, it is evident that Victor is maniacal about his own quest, even to the point of self-destruction, while Walton is willing to realize that there are limits to human endeavor.

TO MRS. SAVILLE: SEPT. 7

Walton writes that he has consented to return if they are not destroyed by the ice, and that he will return "ignorant and disappointed."

TO MRS. SAVILLE: SEPT. 12

The ice has finally broken, and the crew is jubilant because they will soon be returning to England. Frankenstein, however, is still determined to pursue his creature. He tries to get out of bed, thinking that his vengeance will give him strength, but even that small exertion is too great for him, and he faints. After he regains consciousness, he tells Walton that he is still convinced that he was right in not creating a companion for the monster, because the first one "showed unparalleled malignity and selfishness in evil." Victor is still unaware, however, that the monster's hatefulness was caused *not* by something innately evil in the monster, but, instead, by the monster's rejection by both society and his creator. He advises Walton to seek happiness and tranquility and avoid ambition because, he admits, it was his own rabid ambition which first prompted him to create the monster. After this admonition, Victor Frankenstein dies.

Later, Walton hears a horrible noise coming from Victor's cabin. He rushes in, and the scene is so horrifying that he can hardly describe it. In the cabin, hovering over Victor's body, is something "gigantic in stature, uncouth and distorted in its proportions." As it stares at Victor in the coffin, Walton notes that the creature is the most loathsome and hideous thing he has ever encountered. The monster turns to Walton and addresses him with a lament over the body of his deceased creator; the monster is remarkably repentant in this speech. Once again, the monster explains that after the murder of Clerval, he was heartbroken; he pitied Frankenstein, he says, but he was "the slave, not the master, of an impulse which [he] detested yet could not disobey." He tells Walton that Walton has no idea of the "hours and months of misery" which he has endured, "wasting with impotent passions." He explains that he had hoped to meet someone who could ignore his outward deformity and respond to his excellent inner qualities. The monster says that once he was not vile and murderous. Once, he was "filled with sublime and transcendent visions of the beauty and the majesty of goodness." The monster then evokes a vision from *Paradise Lost* and says that "the fallen angel becomes a malignant devil." The monster maintains that he should *not* be thought of as a criminal; he desired only love and friendship, like all creatures, but all of humankind drove him from their doors. The monster says that however much other people despise him, it does not equal the abhorrence which he feels for himself when he gazes on his own deformity. He knows that there is no place for him in the world, and with the remorse that he now feels, he realizes that he shall find peace only in death. He announces his plan: he will build a funeral pyre and die, exulting "in the agony of the torturing flames." Then the monster springs from the cabin window and is "soon borne away by the waves and lost in darkness and distance."

MARY SHELLEY AND ROMANTICISM

Few writers exist outside of the currents of the times in which they live, and Mary Shelley is one of the greatest examples of this concept. She is not only a product of her times, called the Romantic era, but she moved among the greatest talents of that particular time. While the Romantic movement was one which began in Germany with great writers like Goethe, who created the Romantic concept of Faust, a concept which figures so predominantly in Mary Shelley's *Frankenstein*, yet the movement dominated the entirety of Western literature for a significant number of years. In America, some of our greatest talents were those writers associated with this movement – writers such as Herman Melville, Ralph Waldo Emerson, Henry

David Thoreau, Henry Wadsworth Longfellow, and, in particular, Edgar Allan Poe, who seems to bear a particular affinity to such writers as Mary Shelley. Poe's use of the gothic and the bizarre could be said to be a direct descendant of the Frankenstein creation. Among England's greatest Romantic writers are William Words- worth, whom Mary Shelley either quotes from directly, or else para- phrases his metaphors and ideas. In addition, Samuel Taylor Cole- ridge's poem about the Ancient Mariner becomes one of the central metaphors of the novel. And then, of course, Mary Shelley's mother and father, William Godwin and Mary Wollstonecraft, were among the intellectual leaders of the entire movement. Today, Mary Shelley's husband, Percy Bysshe Shelley, lives in the immortality of the Romantic writers, and the great English poet Lord Byron was the person who suggested the idea of writing a terror story to Mary Shelley, a story which later became the genesis of *Frankenstein*.

Since Mary Shelley was so intimate with all of the great minds and talents of the Romantic movement, it is, of course, natural that her work would reflect the Romantic trends. The following discus- sion is not a comprehensive view of key Romantic concepts, but, in- stead, it is intended only as a basic guide and as an explanation for some of the major conventions and some of the devices found in Mary Shelley's novel.

(1) Intuition and Emotion

Perhaps the most dominant characteristic of the Romantic movement was a rejection of the rational and the intellectual in favor of the intuitive and the emotional. For the Romantic, the intellectual and the didactic was to be used for sermons and treatises, and the emotions were the sole province of art; after all, as Mary Shelley points out, the man, or monster (or creature), in her novel felt and sensed things *before* he thought about them. For example, in chapters 11-16, we learn that the monster, on the day that it was first created, was "born" with incipient emotions and feelings, and it was only through great effort that it was able to learn intellectual matters such as reading and writing. Thus, for the Romantic, the subject matter of art should deal with the emotions, and the greatest art was that which had a direct effect on the emotions. Accordingly, every scene in *Frankenstein* deals with some aspect of the emotions – the adoption of underprivileged children, the rejection of a marriage vow in favor of true love, the death of sweet William, and the devotion of Victor and Elizabeth; every scene has characters who are dominated by their emotions. In fact, it is the emotions of these characters which explain much of their seemingly erratic or non-rational behavior.

(2) Setting and Time

Usually in a Romantic story, the setting is in some obscure or unknown place, or at least in a foreign country, and often it is set in some remote place in time. While Mary Shelley's novel is set in contemporary time (because she wanted to emphasize the use of modern science), this is not typical of the usual Romantic concepts. One has only to remember some of the stories of Edgar Allan Poe to see that he set his works in remote, strange places in a time period that is often not even recognizable. Mary Shelley, however, did conform to the Romantic concept of placing her novel and her other fiction in remote Romantic settings. For the Romantic writers, a walking trip through the Swiss Alps was almost a necessity, and thus much of this novel takes place in the Alps. And as noted above, Germany was the center of the Romantic movement; therefore, the creature (or monster) is created in a university in Ingolstadt, Germany, a remote and unknown place to much of the reading public. Later in the novel, when the bride of the monster is to be created, the action takes place on a remote island somewhere off the coast of Scotland (Scotland, too, was a favorite place for Romantic writers to set their stories; many of Sir Walter Scott's, as well as some of Poe's, stories are set in Scotland.). The basic purpose of having a story set in a foreign place was to create a realm that was entirely different from the known world of the reader. After all, for Frankenstein to create a monster in an apartment in the middle of London would not have been as believable – or as exotic – as it was to have him create a monster in the laboratory of a small university in Germany. Above all, the Romantic writer wanted to create new or different worlds so that his readers would concentrate wholly on unusual themes and ideas; thus, the atmosphere of the story is not focused on the mundane aspects of the real world.

(3) Characterization and Verisimilitude

Often the Romantic writer is not interested in creating viable or believable characters. We do not *really* believe in the existence of Frankenstein's monster, yet it has captured the imagination of the Western world and has given rise to numerous literary and cinematic offsprings. Likewise, the various characters in the novel seem to float in and out of reality. We hardly hear of Justine Moritz until Victor's young brother William is killed and, ironically, William, as a character, suddenly appears out of nowhere. The creature, of course, has no real identity, and Robert Walton exists only to present the frame for the novel.

(4) Subject Matter

Romantic writers are often both praised and condemned for emphasizing the strange, the bizarre, the unusual, and the unexpected in their writing, and it is out of this Romantic tradition that we encounter such figures as the monster in *Frankenstein* and Count Dracula (even though the novel *Dracula* was written well past the Romantic era). The Romantics felt that the common and the ordinary had no place in the realm of art. Most Romantic or gothic writers such as Mary Shelley or Edgar Allan Poe eschewed or despised literature that dealt with mundane subjects. One could see such things every day; they were not exciting enough to be the subjects of art.

The purpose of Romantic art was to choose subjects which could affect the reader in a manner which he would not encounter in everyday life. For this reason, the subject matter of many Romantic works dealt with strange creatures (Frankenstein's monster, for example) or a living corpse (the Un-Dead of *Dracula*) or characters in a Poe story who refuse to die, even though they are apparently buried (for example, Lady Madeline Usher in "The Fall of the House of Usher"), or else the Romantic writer chose to relate frightening experiences, using bizarre horrors which he hoped would startle the reader with situations which he had never imagined before. The greatness of *Frankenstein* is due largely to the originality of the concept of a scientist's being able to create a living creature from the dead parts of cadavers and, therefore, being able to assume the godlike power of creating life. In conclusion, then, *Frankenstein* represents the best and the worst elements of the gothic Romantic tale, introducing unexpected events or unexplained actions at any given moment, yet creating a sense of inexorable horror for the reader. After all, a Frankenstein monster cannot and does not exist in the real world, and the final chase in the Arctic is more in keeping with the Romantic temperament of a quest than would be a chase through the streets of London.

THE GOTHIC STORY

Frankenstein represents one of the highest achievements in the literary genre of the gothic horror story. By *gothic*, one means that the author emphasizes the grotesque elements (such as the monster), the mysterious (we are never told exactly how the monster was created or how it could follow Victor Frankenstein about the world), the desolate environment (the story ends in the arctic expanses), the horrible (the many murders), the ghostly (Mary Shelley's evocation of the specter amidst rainstorms and eerie situations), and, ultimately, the abject fear that can be aroused in either the reader or the viewer. Almost everyone today is familiar with such characters as Dr. Frankenstein's monster and Count Dracula, two of today's pop culture horror characters who evolved from the original gothic tradition, which began with *The Castle of Otranto* (1764), and it is probably not an exaggeration to say that most adults in the Western world have been exposed to some type of gothic tale or ghost story. We all know that a gothic story or ghost story will usually have a setting that will be in an old decaying mansion far out in a desolate countryside or in some strange, unfamiliar surroundings, such as Ingolstadt in *Frankenstein* or in Transylvania in *Dracula*. When there is a castle involved, it will be filled with cobwebs, strange noises, bats, and an abundance of secret panels, and corridors, down which persecuted virgins might be running and screaming in terror. This is standard fare; we have either read about such places or have seen them in the movies or on TV. The haunted castle is a classic setting for the gothic story. Frankenstein's monster was created in a weird laboratory where parts of the human body were collected, and almost all accounts of the Dracula legends begin in the desolate region of Transylvania. The author uses every literary trick possible to give us eerie sensations or to make us jump while we are reading if we suddenly hear an unexpected noise. Even the shadows usually seem menacing in these stories, there are often trap doors to swallow us up, and the various underground passages are smelly, slimy, and foul–all of these effects are created for one reason: to give us a sense of the ghostly and the supernatural.

Novels such as *Frankenstein* and *Dracula* utilize many of these aspects of the gothic and are considered to be not just among the earliest examples of gothic horror, but they are also considered to be among the finest examples of the gothic genre in all of literature.

Not surprisingly, all gothic stories have many qualities in common. (1) In addition to the gothic elements, there is a sense of remoteness and a sense of indefiniteness; that is, we are never told exactly where Frankenstein creates his monster, except that it is in Ingolstadt, and how Henry Clerval and the monster get to the coast of Ireland is left unexplained. Thus, parts of *Frankenstein* take place in Geneva, in Ingolstadt, on a Scottish island and, as noted, in Ireland, where Clerval is mysteriously killed. The point here is that these stories take place in remote areas which would be unknown to large numbers of readers. The readers are thus removed from their everyday environments. For example, like *Frankenstein*, Edgar Allan Poe's "Ligeia" is set in an old castle on the Rhine and later in an abbey in the most "remote part of Scotland."

(2) One of the primary aims of the gothic story is to create the single effect of an eerie and ghostly atmosphere, and to do so, the story emphasizes the physical aspects of the various structures — the weird, deep caverns, the bizarre laboratory where the monster is created, or the isolated island where Victor Frankenstein begins his creation of the bride for the monster, as well as the desolated arctic expanses.

(3) In *Frankenstein*, the monster is at first the super-sensitive hero, but being a "monster," he cannot function well in the "normal" world. He makes several attempts to share a super-sensitiveness to the point of maladjustment, but due to his physical appearance, he is constantly rejected.

(4) Often in the gothic story, the characters seem to possess some sort of psychic communication; the creature, for example, seems to always know where his creator is. This communication occurs between a member of the living world and a "living" corpse, or the Un-Dead in *Dracula*, as well as between the created monster and his creator in this novel.

(5) One of the stock elements of the gothic story concerns the possibility of returning to life after one is dead or inhabiting one's own corpse (as in Poe's stories) or being created from dead parts of cadavers (*Frankenstein*). Mary Shelley's novel is the penultimate story that is not a great work of literature, but one which has an idea so unique that it has captured the imagination of most of the Western

world and has given rise to a multiplicity of imitations (even the modern Japanese cinema contains a series of Godzilla films). Never should we consider Mary Shelley's monster to be a sort of deformed "child." Its very countenance suggests something that has returned from the dead. In the same way that Edgar Allan Poe created stories that focused on the return of the entombed and living corpse of the Lady Madeline and the slow re-emergence into life by the enshrouded Lady Ligeia, so Victor Frankenstein's monster at the end of the novel is described by Walton as being shaggy-haired and mummified in visage and deportment, and gigantic in his hideousness.

While it does not apply in particular to *Frankenstein*, many gothic stories place a strong emphasis on the life of the mind after the death of the body. This is also true of the stories associated with the many variations on the Dracula legends, where the focus is upon the continuation of the life of the mind after the body has become one of the Un-Dead.

In conclusion, the gothic story, then, is a type of fiction which uses many varying effects mainly to create a sense of intense terror in the minds of its readers.

THE AMERICAN HORROR FILM AND THE INFLUENCE OF GERMAN EXPRESSIONISM

The influence of German Expressionism on Hollywood films of the Thirties and Forties was tremendous. As an art form, Expressionism is generally considered to be best represented by the works of Van Gogh, Cezanne, and Edward Munch. In painting, Expressionistic art is characterized by a sense of imbalance in the pictorial arrangements in order to achieve distortion; the use of oblique angles and sharp curves; a distortion of line and color, where primary colors are generally used in violent contrast; and a subjective vision of the exterior world. Expressionism also usually incorporates the style of *grisaille*, painting in grey monotone in which objects are often seen only with a suggestion of form and outline without attention to precise detail. The content of Expressionistic art is characterized by its grotesqueness and implausibility. It is a revolt against both Naturalism and Impressionism and has similar counterparts in literature and sculpture.

The enormously creative German cinema in the 1920s was influenced, on the one hand, by the theater of Max Reinhardt, an innovative stage director, and, on the other, it was influenced by Expressionistic art. The advances in lighting techniques, pioneered by Reinhardt, coupled with the rise of Expressionism, was of supreme importance to the experimenting film-makers in post World War I Germany. Most of the actors in the early Expressionistic films were members of Reinhardt's acting company; later, some of them became film directors themselves.

The first great Expressionistic masterpiece in film is *The Cabinet of Dr. Caligari* (1919), written by Hans Janowitz and Carl Mayer, and directed by Robert Wiene. Janowitz was deeply impressed by the work of Paul Wegener, a member of Reinhardt's acting troupe, who had directed the influential *Student of Prague* (1913), in collaboration with the Dane Stellan Rye, and *The Golem* (1915), remade in 1920.

Many of the Expressionistic film-makers in Germany during the Twenties eventually came to the United States. *Caligari* screenwriter Carl Mayer did, as well as Conrad Veidt, the actor who played the somnambulist Cesare in *Caligari*. (Veidt, interestingly enough, was also a member of Reinhardt's acting company.) In addition to these men, the great German film director F. W. Murnau, who directed the first "vampire" film, *Nosferatu* (1922), also went to Hollywood and directed several important films. The innovative Expressionistic cinematographer Karl Freund, who had photographed Wegener's 1920 version of *The Golem* and Fritz Lang's science-fiction classic, *Metropolis* (1927), became one of the most in-demand cinematographers in Hollywood. Freund was the cinematographer of *Dracula* (1931), and he also became an accomplished film director. He directed such horror film masterpieces as *The Mummy* (1932, the first of the series) and *Mad Love* (1934). *Mad Love* starred the now famous, late actor Peter Lorre, who achieved stardom with his powerful portrayal of the child murderer in Fritz Lang's *M* (1931). Fritz Lang, director of *Metropolis* (1927), was the first scheduled director of *The Cabinet of Dr. Caligari*, but he was committed to finish an earlier project. The Expressionist Paul Leni, a set designer for Max Reinhardt, came to the United States in 1927 and directed Conrad Veidt in *The Man Who Laughs* (1928), a silent film produced by Universal Pictures. Leni is important because he singlehandedly developed a new genre of the horror film, juxtaposing scenes which utilized carefully designed and lighted sets and uniquely focused cameras against scenes intended as comic interludes. Leni's unique approach was certainly an influence on James Whale, the director of the first two Frankenstein films. Leni's influence can also be found in the work of Whale's art director for the first two Universal Frankenstein pictures – Charles D. Hall, who was the art director for Leni's *The Man Who Laughs* (1928), *The Cat and the Canary* (1927), and *The Last Warning* (1929). Although Leni's output was slight (he died in Hollywood in 1929), he was an important link between the German and American cinemas.

Thus, the influence of German Expressionism on early Hollywood films is profound and readily evident. Most directors truly concerned about film art knew of the German Expressionist films and learned from them. Upon close examination of the classic horror films of the Thirties, it is discovered that these films are not simply idle "crowd-pleasers," but serious attempts, by concerned individuals, at producing art.

FILMS INFLUENTIAL ON THE PRODUCTION OF THE FILM *FRANKENSTEIN*

The Cabinet of Dr. Caligari (1919). The finest and most famous example of German Expressionism on film. It had a tremendous influence on later Hollywood films and in the history of cinema. It was photographed by Willy Hameister, written by Hans Janowitz and Carl Mayer, and directed by Robert Wiene.

Homunculus (1916). Rarely seen anymore, *Homunculus* was released originally as a six-part serial. Director Otto Rippert and cinematographer Carl Hoffman, one of the finest of the Expressionist photographers, teamed to produce a powerful film which was one of the first films to utilize the lighting effects pioneered by Max Reinhardt.

The Golem (1920). Paul Wegener, once an actor in Max Reinhardt's acting troupe, first directed *The Golem* in 1915, but prints of that version are lost. Wegener was one of the first people to champion the cinema, and he hailed it as the most exciting art form which the world had yet seen. Wegener later became involved in producing

Nazi propaganda films for the Third Reich. In 1920, using a script by Henrik Galeen, with Karl Freund as photographer, Wegener produced the film again, which later became a profound influence on the artistic conception of *Frankenstein*.

Metropolis (1926). The creation of the "robot" in Fritz Lang's classic, with its marvelous optical effects, was an important influence on James Whale's treatment of the creation of the Frankenstein monster. *Metropolis* also premieres the first "mad scientist," who would have an effect on later Frankenstein films and also on many science-fiction films.

Waxworks (1924). Paul Leni, originally a set designer for Max Reinhardt, directed this superb example of German Expressionism, which became an international success. Leni, who was asked by Carl Laemmle, the founder of Universal Pictures, to come to the United States in 1927, did not directly influence *Frankenstein* with this film, but while he was in Hollywood, Leni directed several influential silent pictures and collaborated with art director Charles D. Hall, whom James Whale hired to design the sets for both *Frankenstein* and *The Bride of Frankenstein*.

SELECTED FILMOGRAPHY
Rating Scale

***** A film that is a "must-see"; both artistically brilliant and influential in the history of cinema.

**** An excellent film, distinguished by its innovation on the genre because of its technical brilliance, yet artistically insubstantial in some way.

*** A good film, which, due either to negligence in production or to technical incompetence, resulted in no special distinction; most likely, a work done which is exploitive of the genre; nevertheless, a film that is valuable.

** Mediocre. Technically competent, nostalgically interesting, yet it carries no special distinction whatsoever.

* Poor. A film in which, in addition to the producer's irresponsibility, the directorial integrity is in question.

Frankenstein (1910). No print of this film, produced by Thomas Edison, has been found.

Life without Soul (1915). Another film version of the Frankenstein myth which has been lost.

Frankenstein (1931). *** The most famous of the Frankenstein series, this film was originally scheduled to be directed by Robert Florey and photographed by the famous German Expressionist cinematographer Karl Freund, who had just recently photographed *Dracula* (released St. Valentine's Day, 1931). Florey had chosen Bela Lugosi, fresh from his performance in *Dracula*, to play the part of the monster and was shooting test photography with Freund as the Frankenstein monster in makeup similar to that of the clay-man in Wegener's *Golem*. Replaced by British-born James Whale to direct *Frankenstein*, Florey and Freund went on to make the superb *Murders in the Rue Morgue* (1932). Whale had recently made his directing debut in film with the enormously popular *Journey's End* (1930), a play he had also directed on Broadway. It was Whale, a tall, thin man with an insatiable wit, who chose the quiet, serene British actor Boris Karloff to play the part of the Frankenstein monster. In addition to *Frankenstein*, a classic of the horror genre, Whale also directed *The Bride of Frankenstein* (1935), a film which some critics feel is the finest horror film ever made; *The Old Dark House* (1932); and *The Invisible Man* (1933), among others. For each of the preceding four films, Whale's art director was Charles D. Hall, who had worked with the German Expressionist Paul Leni on Universal's *The Man Who Laughs* (1928), a film which, interestingly, starred Conrad Veidt, the actor who played the part of the somnambulist Cesare in *The Cabinet of Dr. Caligari*.

The Bride of Frankenstein (1935). *** Perhaps the best of all the Frankenstein series, and arguably the finest horror film ever made, *The Bride of Frankenstein* is both a homage to and a

62

parody of the horror film. Whale cast the skeletal Ernest Thesiger as Dr. Pretorious, and Thesiger's performance as the "mad scientist" in the film is the definitive interpretation of that role. In one scene, Dr. Pretorious displays to his associate, Dr. Frankenstein, his "homunculi" – seven creatures which he has created and which he keeps in small jars. The entire scene is grotesquely absurd, yet it is compelling due to Thesiger's intensity. Dressed in black clothes, complete with a medieval alchemist's skullcap, Thesiger's performance is nothing less than stunning. In this production, Whale fashioned the Frankenstein monster into an overt Christ figure – that is, the monster participates in a meal of bread and wine, administered by a hermit dressed in a monk's robe; shortly afterward, he is captured by angry villagers, chained to a stake, and hoisted high into the air to become a bizarre type of Christ. The monster escapes from his prison cell by crashing down the heavy wooden door, and the similarity to iconographical representations of Christ's harrowing Hell is striking. Dr. Pretorious's control over the Frankenstein monster is similar to that of Caligari's over the somnambulist Cesare, and, as in the first Whale production of *Frankenstein*, there are several visual homages to *The Cabinet of Dr. Caligari*. Elsa Lanchester's makeup as the Bride is perhaps the most ridiculous yet the most definitive and imitated in cinema history: her hair is piled on top of her head in a Nefertiti style, and there are two streaks, one on either side of the hairdo, like two lightning bolts. Her response to the Frankenstein monster is horror, and while Whale's direction forces laughter – purposely – the monster, grief-stricken by her rejection, causes the complete destruction of the laboratory, his Bride, Dr. Frankenstein, Pretorious, and himself. In the completely absurd world of Whale's conception, the monster – an outcast, a freak, and a loner – provides the moral center so desperately needed in this horror film.

Son of Frankenstein (1939). **** Like its predecessors, *Son of Frankenstein* features wonderfully Expressionistic sets. It also features a strong script by Willis Cooper. Directed by Rowland V. Lee, *Son of Frankenstein* is an excellent film, yet it lacks the sense of wit and pacing which usually mark Whale's interpretations. Lee's style is slow, precise, and without surprises; it is even somewhat austere. This production introduced, perhaps as a result of the growing fear of Hitler, the extremely efficient, authoritarian bureaucrat Krogh (played by Lionel Atwill) who, as a child, had his arm torn off by the Frankenstein monster and now wears a wooden arm. This film was the last one in which Boris Karloff played the monster.

The Ghost of Frankenstein (1942). *** As the title implies, all that is left of Whale's *Frankenstein* is simply a ghost. Bela Lugosi, as the power-hungry lab assistant, Ygor, gains control of the monster, and, at times, the film approaches the spirit of Expressionistic art – that is, it contains an awareness of human grotesquery. In one scene, the crippled, deformed Ygor leads the monster, played by Lon Chaney, Jr., through a forest of (artificial) dead and twisted trees. Because this film is so superbly Expressionistic, one's concern is with the futures of these two grotesque beings, both struggling in a world that is ostensibly absurd.

Frankenstein Meets the Wolf Man (1943). * Made at the height of World War II, the monster has now become a blind, staggering, mindless robot, perhaps a reflection of the American view of the soldiers in Hitler's army. The Wolf Man was incorporated into the plot ostensibly to capitalize on the popularity of the creature, who had debuted the year before.

House of Frankenstein (1944). * As the popularity of the series declined, Universal (which produced every American Frankenstein picture until 1948) attempted to capture an audience by tossing in every "monster" popular at the time – the Wolf Man, Dracula, and the "mad scientist," as well as the Frankenstein monster.

House of Dracula (1945). *** Directed by Erle C. Kenton, who had directed *Ghost of Frankenstein, House of Dracula* is, despite its title, the last memorable film produced by Universal which featured the Frankenstein monster. In a performance which approaches that of Ernest Thesiger's in *The Bride of Frankenstein,*

64

Onslow Stevens portrays Dr. Edelmann, who is, at first, motivated by a genuine altruistic feeling towards the monster, then is convinced by his beautiful, yet hunchbacked, laboratory assistant (played by Jane Adams) to forsake his attempt to revive the monster. Eventually, Edelmann, who has become infected by a vampire's blood, chooses to revive the monster. The material, however, is never quite under control by director Kenton; the film stumbles and plods along at its own unique pace, while the preposterousness of the action proves to be the very reason why the film works. Despite its "B-movie" status and its illogical plotting, the film is ultimately both humane and moral.

Abbott and Costello Meet Frankenstein (1948). * The last film produced by Universal of the Frankenstein series is best characterized as pathetic. It is still seen because of the continued popularity of the comedians Abbott and Costello, yet their satire is not as sophisticated nor as respectful as is Mel Brook's in *Young Frankenstein* (1974), primarily because Brooks realized that the early films of the Frankenstein series represented a level of achievement and sophistication which most film-makers could only aspire to. Despite the material, the film features a truly sincere performance by the late Lon Chaney, Jr. as the Wolf Man.

I Was a Teenage Frankenstein (1957). * * A film valid only as an interesting piece of sociology. A scientist creates his monster from the parts of dead teenagers, and the creature itself is dressed in a T-shirt and slacks. Not only is the monster a representation of the misunderstood teenager whom James Dean immortalized in *Rebel without a Cause* (1955), but the film itself reflects the public's fear of teenagers, prevalent in the late Fifties and early Sixties.

The Curse of Frankenstein (1957). * * * Hammer Studios of Great Britain entered the horror film market with this production, the first Frankenstein film (along with *I Was a Teenage Frankenstein*) produced in nine years. It also has the distinction of being the first Frankenstein film made in color. Directed by horror film master Terence Fischer, who has directed some of Hammer

Studios' highly successful Dracula films, the film is wonderfully stylized, and it features a gaudy over-abundance of primary colors, actually an Expressionistic device which has trade-marked Hammer films. The film has trouble finding a moral center because the monster is not sympathetic and neither is Frankenstein. The key problem in this film is that it is a bit too violent and vicious—even hysterical—a fault which has hampered and stereotyped all Hammer films of the last two decades.

The Revenge of Frankenstein (1958). * * * While Terence Fisher is a competent horror film director, restraint is not one of his virtues. This film is a good production, and while it presents some fairly interesting innovations by screenwriter Jimmy Sangster, it prefigures the kind of nonchalant production inherent in the worst of the Hammer films.

Frankenstein – 1970 (1958). * * * Like *The Curse of Frankenstein, Frankenstein – 1970* is a bit too vicious and amoral without proper justification; nevertheless, the film is viable. It features a strong performance by Boris Karloff as a disfigured Victor Frankenstein who was a victim of Nazi torture. In this production, Victor intends to animate the monster by means of an atomic device, and the ending has a clever twist.

Frankenstein's Daughter (1959). * Sandra Knight is the created monster in this film, a "low-budget" production which is exploitive of the genre.

The Evil of Frankenstein (1964). * * * * * This film is Hammer Studios' and director Freddie Francis's crowning achievement. Utilizing a script by John Elder (a pseudonym for Anthony Hinds, a frequent Hammer scriptwriter), Francis forsook the Expressionist traditions of the horror film and opted for a simpler style, relying on a Gothic setting and a Romantic mood of sexual depravity and horror. While director Francis—a superb cinematographer whose work is best represented in David Lynch's *The Elephant Man* (1980)—is not the stylist that Terence Fischer is (or even James Whale), he is possessed of a brisk, economical narrative sense. Whereas the creation of the monster was always the central incident in previous Frankenstein films, in this film the creation is not important at all. Francis and Elder rely on the audience's awareness of the tradition and are very concerned with the creator's psychology, an approach to the myth which would reach its apogee in Paul Morrissey's production of *Andy Warhol's Frankenstein* (1974).

Frankenstein Conquers the World and **Frankenstein Meets the Space Monster (both 1965).** * Exploitative films for young adults; the former, a Japanese production starring Nick Adams as the monster; the latter, a "low-budget" picture. Both are forgettable.

Jesse James Meets Frankenstein's Daughter (1965). * Perhaps the worst horror film ever made, along with *Billy the Kid vs. Dracula* (both directed by William Beaudine); the most amazing thing about this film is why – and how – it ever got produced.

Frankenstein Created Woman (1967). * * Terence Fischer teamed with John Elder (Anthony Hinds) for this mediocre film, purely exploitative in intent. In this production, the monster is not hideously deformed, but is played by *Playboy* centerfold Susan Denberg.

Frankenstein Must Be Destroyed (1969). * * Another Hammer Studios' release, this one focuses on a plot that concerns a brain transplant.

Horror of Frankenstein (1970). * * Like the Universal productions, Hammer Studios eventually lost their artistic interest and began simply churning out horror films exploitative of the genre, and *Horror of Frankenstein* is typical.

Dracula vs. Frankenstein (1971). * * A "low-budget" film, memorable because it features the last screen appearances of Lon Chaney, Jr. and J. Carroll Naish. Its special effects were created by Kenneth Strickfaden, the technician who created the laboratory effects for James Whale's productions.

Frankenstein and the Monster from Hell (1972). * * Another Hammer Studios' release.

Frankenstein (1973). * * * The first made-for-TV version, it featured Robert Foxworth as Frankenstein and Bo Svenson as the monster. This production is remarkably close to the novel.

Frankenstein: The True Story (1974). * * * A three-hour version of the myth; produced by Universal-TV, this version, written by Don Bachardy and Christopher Isherwood, despite its claims, does not adhere strictly to the novel. Screenwriters Bachardy and Isherwood create some interesting parallels between Mary Shelley's companions, in Geneva on the night the story was suggested to her, and the characters in the novel (a device which James Whale had also used in *The Bride of Frankenstein*), but this production, despite some superb acting by James Mason, is slow.

Andy Warhol's Frankenstein (1974). * * * * * Written and directed by Andy Warhol's collaborator, Paul Morrissey, this "3-D" version, featuring Udo Kier as Frankenstein, attempts to expose the sexual depravity and horror, as well as the technological irresponsibility, inherent in the Frankenstein myth, something the Hammer productions tried to do but were less successful, mainly because they were directed for a different audience. After years of interpretations of the myth, Morrissey, with an acute awareness of the story inherent for anyone reared in the era of television, was in a position to survey the story and take for granted that his audiences had an awareness of the myth. In Morrissey's vision, there is a fear of science as articulate and disturbing as that in James Whale's original production. Moreover, Morrissey asserts that the creation of life today is left to the whim of the aristocracy, something financed by them for their own perverse interests; as a result, the human body has become simply an object, something to dissect and probe, something that is soulless, worthless, and meaningless. In his vision, the creation mirrors the creator, and the monster is lifeless and as cold as its creator. In this film, science has robbed life of its mystery, and the actions of the creature are at the discretion of its creator. A disturbing film, *Andy Warhol's Frankenstein* is, with the exception of Mel Brooks's film, the ultimate evaluation of the Frankenstein myth.

Young Frankenstein (1974). *** * * *** Mel Brooks's film is both a spoof of Frankenstein films, particularly the early versions, as well as a loving homage. Brooks resurrected some of the original equipment used in Whale's production, and he also hired Kenneth Strickfaden, the electronics expert who created the special effects in the Universal pictures, to revitalize them. Unlike *Andy Warhol's Frankenstein*, released this same year, Brooks's treatment projects a vision of humankind coming to terms with technology.

QUESTIONS FOR REVIEW

1. Discuss Mary Shelley's use of Romantic conventions in this novel.

2. Describe the original personality of Frankenstein's creature and the metamorphosis of its personality.

3. In what ways are Robert Walton and Victor Frankenstein alike?

4. How does the monster learn to read and write?

5. What role does Nature play in this novel?

6. Why does Victor decide not to create a companion for the monster?

7. What are some of the typically Romantic horror conventions which Mary Shelley uses in this novel?

8. How do *The Sorrows of Young Werther*, *Paradise Lost*, and Plutarch's *Lives* influence the monster?

9. Discuss the Romantic Quest and its ironic inversion in this novel.

10. How does Mary Shelley characterize "society," justice, and injustice in relation to Frankenstein's creature?

SELECTED BIBLIOGRAPHY OF WORKS ON GERMAN EXPRESSIONISM AND ITS INFLUENCE ON FILM:

CARTER, HUNTLY. *The Theater of Max Reinhardt*, (1914).

EISNER, LOTTE H. *The Haunted Screen: Expressionism in the German Cinema and the Influence of Max Reinhardt*, (1952, rev. 1965).

KRACAUER, SIEGFRIED. *From Caligari to Hitler: A Psychological History of the German Film*, (1947).

SELECTED BIBLIOGRAPHY OF HORROR FILMS

BAXTER, JOHN. *Hollywood in the Thirties*, (1968).

ELLIS, REED. *A Journey into Darkness: The Art of James Whale's Horror Films* (Doctoral Dissertation; University of Florida) New York: Arno Press, 1980.

EVERSON, WILLIAM K. *Classics of the Horror Film*, (1974).

MILNE, TOM. "One Man Crazy: James Whale," *Sight and Sound* (Vol. 42, No. 3) Summer 1973. pp. 166-70.

PIRIE, DAVID. *A Heritage of Horror: The English Gothic Cinema 1946-1972*, (1973). A good study of the British horror film and its tradition. Pirie also gives an informative history of Hammer Studios and biographies of the major British horror film directors.

STEINBRUNNER, CHRIS, and GOLDBLATT, BURT. *Cinema of the Fantastic*, (1972).

TROPP, MARTIN. *Mary Shelley's Monster,* (1976). A study of both the novel and the conception of the Frankenstein monster in popular culture. The book also provides a filmography and useful bibliography.

SELECTED BIBLIOGRAPHY

General Background to Gothic Fiction:

BATE, WALTER JACKSON. *From Classic to Romantic.* (1946). A study of the development of gothic fiction.

BURKE, EDMUND. *On the Sublime.* (1757). Burke's influential essay emphasized the value of terror and pathos in order to produce a reader's active envolvement.

TOMPKINS, J. M. S. *The Popular Novel in England, 1770-1800.* (1932).

On the Gothic Novel:

BIRKHEAD, EDITH. *The Tale of Terror.* (1921).

PRAZ, MARIO. *The Romantic Agony.* (1933). A study of the history of particular neurotic strains in Romantic literature.

RAILO, EINO. *The Haunted Castle.* (1927). Examines the important motifs of gothic fiction.

SUMMERS, MONTAGUE. *The Gothic Quest.* (1939). An intensive study of the genre up to 1800.

VARMA, P. DAVENDRA. *The Gothic Flame.* (1956). The best recent study.

Biography:

GRYLLS, R. GLYNN. *Mary Shelley, A Biography.* (1938).

Critical Works on Frankenstein:

ALDISS, BRIAN W. *Billion Year Spree.* (1973). A study of the development of science-fiction; Aldiss views *Frankenstein* as the first science-fiction novel.

FLORESCU, RADU. *In Search of Frankenstein.* (1975).

WOLF, LEONARD, ed. *The Annotated Frankenstein.* (1977). Provides the original text of *Frankenstein* and includes extensive annotations.

Frankenstein Genealogy

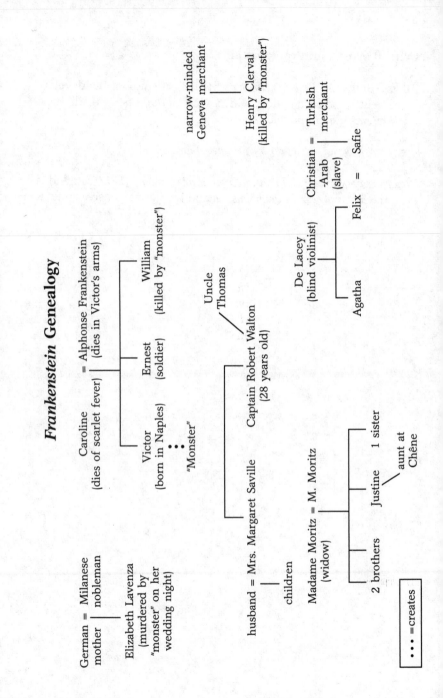

German = Milanese mother nobleman

Caroline (dies of scarlet fever) = Alphonse Frankenstein (dies in Victor's arms)

narrow-minded Geneva merchant

Henry Clerval (killed by "monster")

Elizabeth Lavenza (murdered by "monster" on her wedding night)

Victor (born in Naples)

•••• "Monster"

Ernest (soldier)

William (killed by "monster")

Uncle Thomas

Captain Robert Walton (28 years old)

De Lacey (blind violinist)

Christian = Turkish -Arab merchant (slave)

Agatha   Felix = Safie

husband = Mrs. Margaret Saville

children

Madame Moritz = M. Moritz (widow)

2 brothers   Justine   1 sister
                           aunt at Chêne

•••• =creates